FIT *to* PRINT

The Canadian Student's Guide to Essay Writing

Joanne Buckley

University of Western Ontario

HBJ

Harcourt Brace Jovanovich

Toronto   Orlando   San Diego   London   Sydney

Copyright © 1987 by Harcourt Brace Jovanovich Canada Inc.,
55 Horner Avenue, Toronto, Ontario M8Z 4X6

Requests for permission to make copies of any part of the work should be mailed to: Permissions, University and Professional Division, Harcourt Brace Jovanovich, Canada, 55 Horner Avenue, Toronto, Ontario M8Z 4X6

Canadian Cataloguing in Publication Data

Buckley, Joanne Lorna, 1953-
   Fit to Print

Includes index.
ISBN 0-7747-3079-X

1. Report writing. 2. English language—Rhetoric.
I. Title.

LB2369.B83 1987   808'.02   C87-093869-X

Design: Jack Steiner Graphic Design
Cover Illustration: Peter Nagy

Printed and bound in Canada
  2 3 4 5 91 90 89 88

Contents

Preface

FIT TO PRINT addresses the problems of essay writing encountered by most students today at the university, college, and secondary levels. Students in the humanities and in the social sciences will find this text particularly useful because it emphasizes the different types of essays required by these disciplines: the research essay, the essay exam, and the book review.

FIT TO PRINT is not another stuffy, prescriptive composition and grammar text: it offers practical advice on how to organize an essay, it uses illustrations from student work in various disciplines, and it provides a versatile approach to composition that may be used by an instructor teaching in a classroom or by a student seeking a self-help guide. The step-by-step approach provides exercises along the way to hone particular skills in essay organization and craftsmanship. In addition, there are sections on specific grammatical problems, revising, and editing to help the student or the teacher overcome certain recurring difficulties in grammar and composition.

To make this guide useful to those of you seeking specific assistance, I have deliberately dealt with the difficulties of diagnosing your own errors and weaknesses. At the same time, the text includes some fundamental reference tools, such as a glossary of usage and a guide through grammatical jargon.

If language is truly the garment of thought, as Aristotle says, then a writer must learn to "dress for success" by choosing words that suit his or her style as well as the topic chosen. Writing that makes a good impression is a pleasure not only for the reader, but also for the writer.

Acknowledgments

I would like to thank all those people who helped with the writing of this book. John Smallbridge, Allan Gedalof, Stan Dragland, Mary Louise Young Collins, Stephen Adams, Jim Good, Ross Woodman, Dick Shroyer, and Alan Bailin all supplied me with useful suggestions and assistance. My thanks also to people from other departments at the University of Western Ontario who supplied me with sample essays, examinations, and other student work. Chief among these were Tom Sea, Bruce Bowden, Keith Fleming, and Cathy Sims of the History department, Carl Grindstaff and Ben Singer of the Sociology department, and M. W. Westmacott of Political Science. Thanks also go to Walter Zimmerman, Beverly Sweezie, and my reviewers, Gerald Lynch, David O'Rourke, Brock Shoveller, Greg Pyrcz, as well as many helpful students and friends whose ideas were invaluable. My editors, Heather McWhinney, Bruce Erskine, and Julie Canton, worked as hard as I did to make this book presentable. I appreciate, in particular, the research essay that Michelle Monteyne gave me permission to include. Finally, I would like to thank Mary Buckley for her support and David Gates for his wit, taste, and companionship, without which this book would be called "Fit to be Tied," instead of *Fit to Print*.

Introduction— Defining The Essay

> One's subject is in the merest grain, the speck of truth, of beauty, of reality, scarce visible to the common eye.
>
> *Henry James*

■ If At First You Don't Succeed ...

The essay, as any dictionary will tell you, is an attempt. This definition itself ought to be reassuring if you have ever worried about how you would be able to write an essay. You can't fail as long as what you write is a sincere attempt to come to terms with a particular subject. The finished essay succeeds insofar as it is an honest attempt to elucidate some aspect of your topic.

An essay need not fail as long as your ideas are treated fairly, honestly, and in a spirit of thorough and intensive investigation—and you have communicated these ideas to the reader! If the essay seems an especially burdensome assignment, it may be because most of us are not accustomed to independent thought. Try to think of the essay as an opportunity to stretch your intellectual muscles and to think your own thoughts.

To write an essay is to engage in a creative process, to bring an idea to life. The essay itself, however, is a finished product, not a record of the process by which you wrote it.

Whether you are writing an expository essay (meant to explain something), or a persuasive essay (meant to argue something), the essay's chief purpose is to present a thesis that focuses your ideas and conveys them to the reader in a way that shows their worth and their validity. Depending on the occasion, an essay may be formal or informal; however, academic writing usually demands formality. Depending on the nature of the assignment, the essay may be a product of reasoning or a combination of reasoning and research.

This text deals both with the essentials of essay writing and with the variations expected in different kinds of assignments. Skim its contents first to acquaint yourself with the most important steps of essay writing. If you are unfamiliar with the basic requirements of the essay, pay special attention to Parts I, II, and III. If you are unsure of the specific guidelines for a particular kind of essay, check the pertinent section in Part IV. Then, as you write your next essay, use this book as a step-by-step guide. It will provide helpful suggestions on how to organize your thinking, and how to present your material in the most effective manner.

Remember that the essay is an attempt to think out your ideas in a structured way. Each attempt will teach you more about how the process works for you.

■ Try, Try Again

As you plan and write the essay, you will be trying various ideas on for size. The process of writing an essay involves finding some part of a large topic that fits your attitude and interest in the subject. Compromise is essential. The essay must fit both you and the topic: it will show you and the reader what you know and what you have yet to learn. For best results, choose a topic in which you have some personal stake. Make sure that you can treat the topic satisfactorily within the required word limit and within the time constraints of the assignment.

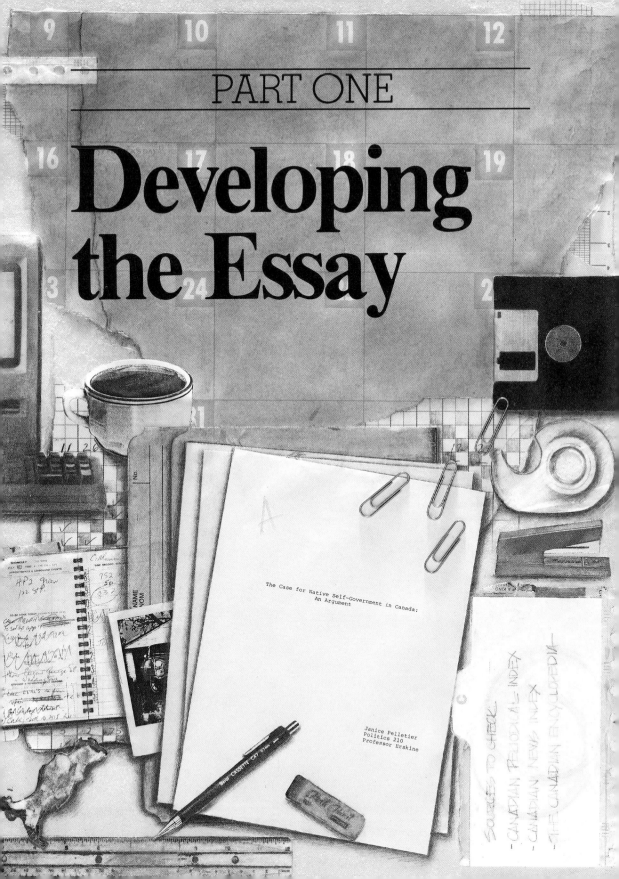

PART ONE

Developing the Essay

The Case for Native Self-Government in Canada:
An Argument

Janice Pelletier
Politics 210
Professor Erskine

Devising a Thesis

My essays . . . come home to men's business and bosoms.

Francis Bacon

Usually when you begin to write an essay, you will have in mind a broad area of concentration, or a fundamental topic that you mean to explore. To write a successful essay, you must find the focal point of your discussion—the centre of your thought, from which the points you make may radiate outward. This focal point is the thesis statement.

Topics are only the starting point for your thinking. They tell you only the general area of investigation. Whether a topic is given to you by the instructor, or whether you find your own, the topic must still be narrowed down to serve as the focus of your paper. Like a target in the middle of a dartboard, the thesis statement is the centre that holds your argument together. An essay succeeds because the point to be made is directly on target, and the significance of the point is firmly established.

■ Discovering a Topic

If your instructor has not suggested areas for exploration, you will have to create your own, usually subject to his or her approval. This process need not be drudgery; it gives you the opportunity to explore your own interest in the subject.

The following are some suggestions for finding a general topic or area of interest:

1. Skim the index and table of contents of any books mentioned in class as useful sources.
2. Skim through class notes and text for ideas that catch your imagination.
3. Ask questions about the meaning and value of the subject.
4. Always write down ideas as you go along.

■ Shopping for a Thesis Statement

Often, you will be given a general topic with instructions to narrow it down. Remember, though, a topic is only a general idea in need of development. Suppose you were asked in an Administrative Studies course to write an essay of 2500–3000 words about productivity growth in Japan. Obviously, this is a broad subject that could yield several promising thesis statements. By itself, however, it is just a phrase, unconnected to any meaning or value. Keep this example in mind as you read through the following tips on developing a specific thesis statement.

Consider the writing situation

When you develop a topic, keep these determining factors in mind:

1. your interests, strengths, and weaknesses
2. the reader's expectations
3. the restrictions of the assignment

Use whatever you have at your disposal

1. supplemental bibliographies you may have been given
2. advice from the instructor
3. material from the course itself
4. your native wit
5. library materials—books, journals, and audio-visual materials

Ask questions about the general topic

Your first question with regard to our sample might be "What about it?" Your sources, both in class and out, may have revealed to you that Japanese productivity growth has greatly surpassed that of Canada since World War II.

Your next question might be "Why?", suggesting a cause and effect development, or even "How?", suggesting an argument based on classification (the breakdown of ideas into categories) or on process (the orderly presentation of steps). Refer also to the chapter "Choosing a Pattern of Argument" for some suggested approaches to topic development.

Consider your topic in conjunction with something else

Try joining your topic to these conjunctions: "and," "or," "but," "so." These linking words should give you some idea of what might be productively attached to your topic to yield interesting results.

"And," for example, might help generate other things to be compared with your subject: Japanese productivity and Canadian productivity, for instance.

"Or" might lead you to consider a controversy about the causes of Japanese productivity: advanced technology or employee motivation, for example.

"But" might allow you to refute the position of a particular authority on the subject, or to prove that the rate of productivity growth in Japan's case is more a result of the stage of its industrial development than of superior technology or administration.

Consider key words that form part of the topic

Ask yourself about the nuances of the question or topic for discussion: is there ambiguity or potential for development in the wording of the question? Instructors setting topics usually have only a sketchy idea in mind; try to see as much as or more in the topic than they have.

In our brief example, one word to which this tactic might apply is "productivity" itself. To develop your topic, you might investigate what particular areas are most productive, to find a clue for your response. You might also want to explore exactly what is meant by "growth." Does it mean increased profits, expansion in number of products, or development of new products?

Consult your own taste

Your taste in topics should be consulted before you settle on anything. About the only serious mistake you can make is to choose a topic simply because it looks easier than the others. A challenge is often the best choice since it allows you to ponder the topic rather than assuming, probably incorrectly, that the main point is clear or the answer is obvious.

Try on the topic before you decide

Always play with the topic before you work on it. Play with ideas by scratching them down haphazardly on a sheet of paper without regard (for now) to problems of order or clarity. This kind of unstructured thinking will open up the possibilities of the question or the topic for you in a way that no amount of tidy compartmentalizing can.

■ A Working Thesis vs. a Polished Thesis Statement

If you follow the guidelines above, you should be able to arrive at a narrow focus for your paper. But even a thesis statement should be subject to revision. Because it is normally part of the introduction to a paper, writers often mistakenly assume that it should be written first. In fact, your real thesis statement may only emerge after you have made several false starts.

Since you have to start somewhere, begin with a working thesis. It will allow you to consider your material from a tentative point of view. If you find that the evidence begins to contradict it, or you no longer consider it the centre of your discussion, redefine your statement to suit the new circumstances.

The thesis statement that appears in your finished introduction will be the best description of what you are trying to prove and of how you propose to do it. For example, your thesis statement on the subject of Japanese productivity growth might look like this:

The enormous increase recorded in productivity growth in Japan in the past ten years is largely the result of new theories of employee relations that have been developed in Japanese industry.

■ What to Look for in a Thesis Statement

Personal conviction

No writing of any power is ever possible without commitment to the subject. No motivation is ever as pressing as the need to say something on a subject that matters urgently to you. Your first task is to find an approach to the topic capable of moving you to care and to work and to write. If you can find such an approach, the process of writing—the reading, the thinking, even the reworking of your thoughts—will be carried along by the desire to know and not only by the demand to complete an assignment.

Pertinence

An essay should not be a trivial pursuit. It should matter to you and to its reader. As you shape your thesis statement, keep the *value* of your subject in mind. When selecting a point of view, allow yourself to think about its broader implications, even if there is no place to include all of these in the essay itself. You don't have to tell readers how relevant your topic is, but you should believe it, and you should be able to show it. Ensuring that your perspective is new and making your point of view matter to your reader are fundamental requirements.

Proportion

The thesis statement indicates what size the essay will be in its finished form. A well-measured thesis statement is snug, not loose, in its fit. If it does not fit properly, the arguments that follow may sag. To ensure a good fit between thesis statement and essay, ask questions. Ask yourself if there is room in a 1500-word essay to discuss the causes of the French Revolution. If not, then trim the thesis statement to fit: e.g., The publication of *Le Contrat Social* was an important cause of the French Revolution.

Precision

As in a legal contract, the essay is the delivery of promises made in its thesis statement. And, as with all such contracts, the issues to be dealt with must be clarified at the outset. Make sure before undertaking an essay topic that you have made clear to your readers both what your essay will do *and* what it will *not* do. Feel free to announce (without apologies) in or near the thesis statement what the limits of your treatment of the subject are.

Point

Not only should your thesis statement have a point to make, it must point in a particular direction. A useful addition to the thesis statement itself is the "route map." The route map informs readers of the highlights of the journey they are about to make. For instance, in a sociology essay comparing the changing attitudes toward women in advertisements from the 1940s to the 1980s, as reflected in two issues of the same magazine, you can briefly outline the steps in your discussion:

> *Three major changes can be noted in the presentation of female figures: women are shown less often in domestic situations; women are more often featured as authority figures; and women are more often shown in active, rather than passive, roles.*

Such a statement contains the direction of the entire essay in miniature and points toward the arguments to follow.

Now that you have a thesis statement . . .

Use your thesis statement as the springboard for your outline. Keep it in mind as you develop your thought. With your thesis statement on paper, you are now ready to design an outline.

EXERCISES

1. Develop a focus for the following topics, using some of the techniques listed above. *Hint:* Each is meant to be the subject of a 1500-word essay in the discipline suggested.
   a. women in the Canadian work force (Sociology)
   b. Soviet military intervention in Afghanistan (Political Science)
   c. the ode (English)
   d. volleyball (or another sport) (Physical Education)
   e. national unity (Political Science)
   f. treatment of native peoples (History)
   g. Greek tragedy (Classical Studies)
   h. media and advertising (Sociology)
   i. the ethics of abortion (Philosophy)

2. Examine some of your past essays to see if the thesis statements you have written have narrowed the topic down sufficiently. Try rewriting them to give them more focus.

PART TWO
Designing the Essay

The Case for Native Self-Government in Canada:
An Argument

Janice Pelletier
Politics 210
Professor Erskine

Designing an Outline

Form ever follows function.

Louis Henri Sullivan

Once you have decided upon your topic and determined your thesis statement, you need an outline.

Never attempt to write an essay without some kind of outline — whether it be a formal, detailed itinerary or a hastily jotted map showing your destination, your direction, and the stops you wish to make along the way.

When preparing an outline, remember that it is only a sketch of your paper. The final design of the essay may be quite different from what you originally intended. A sketch does not need to be perfect. The outline is meant to help you write the paper, not to restrict your line of thought. Keep the outline flexible so that you can tinker with it as you go along. It is simply a tentative blueprint, a description of the contents of your paper, rather than a prescription of its requirements.

■ Make a Table of Contents

Think of the outline as your own flexible table of contents. It is, after all, your note to yourself, your reminder of what details you wish to include, and what arguments you want to make. Like a table of contents, the outline labels what the reader may expect to find contained in the work itself.

Take a look at the Table of Contents of this book for a moment to see what information can be gleaned from it. Not only does it tell you *what* is included in the book, it tells you what the major and minor divisions of the work are. For instance, you will find the chapter entitled "Devising a Thesis" under the part heading *Developing the Essay*.

In other words, the table of contents gives the reader a sense of the book's dimensions. You see, for example, that the book you are holding in your hand has six major parts, each of which is divided into a number of chapters. Not only does this give you a sense of the work's overall shape, but also of the size of each component, and, at the same time, a sense of the orderly arrangement of its position within the work. What follows is not a set of rules for composing outlines, but a series of suggestions about what they may contain.

To make your outline as useful and as organized as a table of contents, keep the following steps in mind:

■ Sort Through Your Ideas

1. Make sure you have established your pivotal points: the thesis statement and purpose.

Use your thesis statement (subject to revision) and your selected purpose as the launching points for your outline. From them will emanate all the ideas, arguments, facts, and figures you have gathered.

2. Gather your notes.

With your tentative thesis statement on paper in front of you, gather your tentative remarks, your research, and your questions about the topic. One good way to take notes is to list separate ideas on cue cards (remembering to include sources, if any). This way, you can shuffle or discard material easily.

Keeping your purpose in mind, organize the material you have selected, discarding any information not strictly related to it. If you are discussing kinds of stage props, for instance, don't include material on their development in the history of the theatre.

3. Classify your material.

Decide how many steps your argument contains. Then classify your notes accordingly. If, for example, you mean to consider three reasons that Japanese businesses outrank their Canadian counterparts, decide in which of the three discussions to include a statistic about productivity growth.

4. Order your material in a logical way.

This process demands that you decide at what point a particular argument should be mentioned. Here you must decide what your opening argument, your follow up, and your last word should be. Keep in mind the tried-and-true notion that a strong point is best placed at the beginning or ending of an essay. Keep in mind, too, that some of your organizational decisions are dependent upon the pattern of argument you selected at the outset. If you know, for instance, that your reader will need to understand your definition of a crown corporation to get the most out of your essay, put it where it will be most accessible. Or, if you are explaining a process, the reader must be able to follow it step by step.

5. Rank your points according to their importance.

Sorting your ideas according to rank means deciding whether an item has a major role or merely a minor one to play. The ranking itself will give you an excellent idea of what you have to say, and of how developed your thought is. Where you have much to add or to explain, the idea is vital and may serve as a significant part of your argument; where your idea is almost all you have to say on the subject, you may relegate the point to a minor status.

In order to rank your ideas, assign them numbers or letters, beginning perhaps with capital Roman numerals for major sections, moving to capital letters for important supporting sections, through to Arabic numbers for less important support material, to small letters for the minor details. The points you are making are primary in rank; the support you gather for them is secondary.

Example

I. Japan outranks Canada in productivity for two reasons.

   A. Japanese companies are especially concerned with employee relations.
      (REASON # 1)

      1. Employees are often hired for life, not for limited periods, as often is
         done in Canada.
      2. Employees are given greater benefits and security than in Canadian
         companies.
         a. They are encouraged to participate in decisions more often than is
            the case in Canada.
         b. Their jobs are usually more stable than ours, though lower wages
            are sometimes the result.
         c. Japanese workers are treated like family members, rather than as
            employees.

   B. Japanese companies place special emphasis on technological advance-
      ments. (REASON # 2)

      1. Technological advancement has permitted more efficient quality con-
         trol.
         a. "Computerized" and "robotized" assembly lines have decreased
            the margin of error.
            . . . and so on

The notation does not matter particularly, but it should permit you to see *at
a glance* the relative scope of the point you are making. A carefully ranked
outline will show you the ideas within ideas.

■ Tailor the Outline

As you outline, you may well notice some rags and tatters among your notes,
bits of research material that seemed valuable at the time you took your notes,
though they now seem unrelated to the development of your thought. If you
cannot use these scraps in the final fabric of your argument, do not hesitate to
toss them out. Remember that one of the main functions of the outline is to
show you how well the material you have gathered actually fits the viewpoint
you have chosen. Each point of the outline ought to represent an area that you
can fill with developed thoughts, facts, and evidence. If you find that all you
have to say on a particular point can be fleshed out in one sentence, then you
must find a way to incorporate that small point into another place in your
argument or perhaps eliminate it altogether. What isn't useful or appropriate
for your thesis statement should be left behind.

This outline shows a short persuasive essay developed by examples, definition, classification, and even comparison/contrast. Basically, the essay consists
of three arguments to defend the thesis, plus supporting arguments. These
patterns of argument will be discussed in the next chapter.

Note that each section has a small thesis statement (or topic sentence) of its own. These are best written as sentences in the outline to ensure clarity. Note also that the subdivisions allow you to see at a glance what items have the most support (and conversely, what might be in need of greater support or development).

A sample student outline

THESIS STATEMENT: "Fighting is essential in pro hockey."

PURPOSE: To persuade a sceptical reader.

I. INTRODUCTION: Some fighting is essential in pro hockey (statement of thesis).

Preview
A. Fighting provides excitement for spectators.
B. Fighting increases competitive spirit.
C. Fighting allows a healthy release of tension.

II. ARGUMENT: Fighting is one of the main attractions of the game for players and viewers.
   A. **Example:** Sports highlights often feature fights.

   B. **Comparison/Contrast:** Hockey's popularity is in part due to the thrill of combat. (Even sports like tennis rely, to some extent, on players' tantrums for their excitement.)

III. ARGUMENT: Fighting promotes the competitive spirit of the sport.
   A. **Example:** Canada/Russia hockey games promote strong feelings of competition, better expressed in sports than in political manoeuvres.
   B. **Definition:** Team sports necessarily involve competition, reward, and punishment: penalties are part of the way the game is played.
   C. **Classification:** The penalty system is designed to control the severity of fighting. There are many kinds of penalties, depending on the severity of the offence. These penalties are meant to discourage excessive fighting and misconduct, but not to banish them.

IV. ARGUMENT: Fighting allows a healthy release of tension.
   A. **Definition:** Not all fighting is necessarily destructive or gratuitously violent.

   1. Most fighting is playful. Injuries are accidents, not the direct result of fighting.

2. Viewers are given the vicarious (and harmless) pleasure of engaging in a fight.
3. Fighting allows "scores to be settled" in a controlled environment under the supervision of coaches and referees.

V. CONCLUSION: Fighting plays a necessary role in pro hockey.

EXERCISES

1. Develop outlines, complete with thesis statements, for the following topics:
   a. censorship in movies
   b. free trade
   c. student housing problems
   d. TV evangelism
   e. euthanasia
   f. the Yuppie movement — modern materialism
   g. the need for improved sex education
   h. literature: popular novels vs. classics

2. Reread an essay you have written for a course in the past and sketch an outline of its structure. Is each section clearly delineated? Is adequate support given for each point that you raise? Is the movement of the paper logical and easy to follow? Would you do anything differently in light of the outline you have produced?

Choosing a Pattern of Argument

Rightly to be great
Is not to stir without great argument.

William Shakespeare

After you have established your thesis statement and made your outline, you need to choose the pattern or patterns of argument that will do it justice. Usually an essay will demand several patterns in support of its thesis, as the sample outline in the preceding chapter demonstrates. In order to support your thesis with a similar variety of arguments, you must look for methods by which to direct your thought. The following tactics may serve as structural guidelines or blueprints for your thought.

Definition/Description
Example
Classification
Process
Comparison/Contrast
Cause/Effect
Narration

These patterns cannot be entirely separated from each other. Usually, a writer will use several patterns to develop one essay. Refer, for example, to the outline in the preceding chapter. It uses many different kinds of argument, including definition, classification, comparison/contrast, and example.

A paragraph that defines "love," for example, may contrast it to "lust" in order to make the distinction clearer. Or it may provide examples of kinds of love to illustrate the breadth of the definition. It may, perhaps, distinguish between erotic love and the Christian concept of charity.

The patterns listed below should offer you some inspiration when you get stuck in the process of outlining your thought. Refer to this section when you need help in the amplification of an argument.

■ Definition/Description

Definition suggests the use of a dictionary to define a term explicitly. This tactic ensures that there is a general consensus between writer and readers as to the term's meaning in the context of the essay.

Although dictionary definitions are important, don't rely too heavily on them. Belabouring a definition already familiar to your readers may alienate them: it may sound condescending. Furthermore, a critical reader will be more concerned with what you *make* of a definition than with its arbitrary recital. If you do cite a dictionary definition, make sure that you use it to make a point.

What is needed in a useful definition? First, it must supply the reader with characteristics that describe something. Occasionally, it may describe by way of comparison/contrast, by showing what the thing is not. And, it may give some enlightening history of the term, showing how it came to have the meaning it has. It may then show what something does, in order to describe more concretely what it is. Lastly, it may give an example, meant to epitomize the nature of the thing described.

Example

Love is patient; love is kind and envies no one. Love is never boastful, nor conceited, nor rude; never selfish, not quick to take offence. Love keeps no score of wrongs; does not gloat over other men's sins, but delights in the truth. There is nothing love cannot face; there is no limit to its faith, its hope, and its endurance.
I Corinthians 13, The New English Bible

This definition makes love a concrete, visible entity, capable of action, rather than merely an abstract concept.

■ Example

Because readers usually find it easier to understand what they can picture, examples are often the best means of amplifying an argument. Whether you use an extended example, meant to illustrate your general point in a series of specific ways, or whether you use a variety of small examples to achieve the same end, examples lend support to your argument.

Example

Love, although it is generally considered the most joyful and pleasurable human emotion, is nonetheless often associated with illness and with pain. In the words of a Renaissance poet, Samuel Daniel, for example, "Love is a sickness full of woes, / All remedies refusing." And Shakespeare's Cleopatra herself declares, "I am sick of love." Yet, while Abraham Cowley warns, "A mighty pain to love it is," Dryden hastens to remind the reader that the "Pains of love be sweeter far / Than all other pleasures are."

This series of undeveloped examples shows a variety of authors who together support the point being made.

■ Classification

In order to explain something more precisely, a writer often has recourse to methods of classification, by which he or she can make necessary distinctions within a subject area. Classifying different parts of a subject involves making decisions about what belongs where. A large subject may be divided into smaller, more manageable sections to make important distinctions clear. In order for classification to work convincingly, the reader must be assured that the categories are tidy, include everything essential, and do not substantially overlap.

Example

> *Love is a word used to describe a range of quite different emotions. Erich Fromm, in* The Art of Loving, *discusses five distinct kinds of love: brotherly love, motherly love, erotic love, self-love, and the love of God. Each of these kinds of love is directed towards a different object: the first towards one's fellows; the second towards offspring; the third towards a sexual partner, the fourth towards oneself; the last towards the creator.*

This classification, borrowed from Fromm, illustrates that love is a broad rather than a specific term.

■ Process

It is often necessary in the course of an essay to explain how to do something, or how something works. When describing a process, think of yourself as a teacher. It is part of your job to supply your readers with all the information they require to understand a given process without confusion. At the same time, you must be careful to assess their level of understanding accurately, if you are to avoid writing that is boring or condescending. It is also part of your job to present the material in a logical step-by-step manner, so that the reader is spared needless cross-referencing and rereading. Be prepared to check the process you have described to see if its steps can be easily followed.

Example

> *When two people fall in love, they often seem to pass through a number of quite predictable stages. They begin, as animals do, by courting each other, perhaps preening and displaying their best features in an effort to attract each other. This courting phase lasts just long enough for the participants to get one another's attention. In the next stage, the romantic phase, they begin to idealize, endowing each other with almost supernatural powers and attractions. Finally, they begin to spend time with each other, having meals together and sharing experiences. The sharing phase, while it lasts, allows the lovers to revel in one another without yet discovering the imperfections in the beloved.*

This paragraph uses transitions such as "in the next stage," and "finally," as well as words like "this" to divide the process into clear stages of development.

■ Comparison/Contrast

Comparisons are an essential part of expository writing. No pattern of argument is more common on examination questions, for instance, than comparison/contrast.

A comparison includes both similarities and differences. When you contrast, however, you focus exclusively on the differences between things.

When comparing, keep the overall structure in mind. You may present first one thing and then the other, or you may present the two things in combination. Alternating between the two is best if the material to be covered is complex or lengthy.

Example

Love in poetry and in psychology textbooks has often been compared to mania. Both involve elation and grandiose thinking, loss of interest in much of one's ordinary daily life, loss of appetite, loss of sleep, uncharacteristic risk-taking, and a feeling of euphoria. And, like mania, romantic attachments do seem to have some effect on neurochemical activity in the human body—so much so, that some drugs used to alter the chemistry of the brain are helpful in treating the depression resulting from a broken heart.

The similarities between love and mania are listed *together* in this paragraph. Note how the parallels between them are developed.

◼ Cause and Effect

This pattern traces the relationship between the cause of an event or a condition and its results. When seeking to develop an argument by tracing causes and their effects, keep in mind two potential dangers. First, beware of trusting the idea of causality too much. Simply because one thing follows another chronologically does not mean that the second event was caused by the first.

Secondly, do not limit effects to one cause alone. Usually more than one determinant brings about an event or a trend. Don't wear blinkers in your zeal to establish connections.

Example

Love, and its accompanying courting rituals, often cause bizarre behaviour. Nor is such behaviour confined to humans, as James Thurber relates in "Courtship Through the Ages." There he speaks of the "Courtship of Animals, ...[or] the sorrowful lengths to which all males must go to arouse the interest of a lady." He then goes on to suggest that love (or its biological equivalent in animals) has been the cause of many strange courtship rituals. He speculates, for example, that "[i]n ancient times man himself, observing the ways of the peacock, probably tried vibrating his whiskers to make a rustling sound." When this tactic was unsuccessful, Thurber observes, "[h]e had to go in for something else; so, among other things, he went in for gifts." While it may be extreme to declare love the cause of peculiar courtship rituals, Thurber does have a point. Behaviour is often strangely altered, in animals and in humans, by the exigencies of courtship.

◼ Narration

Telling a story, like telling a good joke, is hard to do. You narrate, or tell a story, in a piece of expository writing in order to bring your argument to life.

To be effective, the narrative you use in an essay should contain carefully selected, telling details—enough to be vivid, not so many that it is boring. The narrative must be well timed: it should draw your reader into your writing, or graphically illustrate a point you are making. It should hold the reader's attention: do not expand the story endlessly with "and then . . . and then . . . and then."

Use narration sparingly in essay writing. Most commonly you will find it used to relate case studies, brief anecdotes, and extended examples.

Example

Emma is a nineteen-year-old student who sees a counsellor once a week to discuss her problems in getting over her broken relationship with Charles. She is frequently despondent, often bursting into tears. She complains that she is unable to sleep and that her powers of concentration in class have diminished, so much so that her grades have fallen from B's to C's in the course of the term.

This paragraph offers a case study to illustrate the pain and psychological symptoms of grief for a lost love.

■ Tips on Choosing the Right Pattern

Your choice of pattern may depend to some extent on your subject. In English, for example, one of the most common patterns is *Comparison/Contrast*. In Political Science and Sociology, you may find yourself most often choosing *Definition* or *Classification*. History makes most use of the *Cause/Effect* pattern. The most common pattern in all writing is *Example*. Choose your pattern wisely; keep its relevance to the overall thesis statement always in mind.

EXERCISES

1. Develop the following thesis statements by using at least two appropriate patterns of argument:
   a. Outdoor team sports are good for more than just your muscles.
   b. Cooking for company is challenging, but not difficult.
   c. Video games are (or are not) a waste of time.
   d. Business courses help prepare students for a competitive environment.
   e. Watching "Pay TV" is a fine alternative to going to the movies.

2. Develop a thesis statement for one of the following topics:
   a. young love
   b. Japanese–Canadian economic competitiveness

   Next, for each topic develop a short introductory paragraph ending with the thesis statement.
   Go through the patterns of argument listed and decide which methods would be most appropriate to develop your thesis statement.
   Then, outline the essay.

3. Analyze the patterns of argument in a paper you have written in the past. What are your most common patterns? What patterns could be used more effectively?

PART THREE
Drafting the Essay

The Case for Native Self-Government in Canada:
An Argument

Janice Pelletier
Politics 210
Professor Erskine

SOURCES TO CHECK:
- CANADIAN PERIODICAL INDEX
- CANADIAN NEWS INDEX
- THE CANADIAN ENCYCLOPEDIA

Shaping the Essay

> You must jot down ideas as they occur to you. The jotting is simplicity itself—it is the occurring which is difficult.
>
> *Stephen Leacock*

As you develop your outline from its bare structure to its fully dressed form, remember that the shape of the essay is in your hands. Though there are guidelines you can follow, the essay is not a form to be filled in. You create the form itself, by selecting what is included and what is left out.

■ The First Draft

To make the first draft of your essay easier to write, keep the following advice in mind:

Write while you think, not after

To move from outline to essay, you need to develop your thought. This development does not involve long delays and cautious planning. Writing is not the expression of thought; it is thought itself. To avoid getting tangled up in a web of confusion, or worse, procrastination, write as you think, rather than after you have thought. Putting pen to paper, even in an unpolished way, will help you overcome the terror of the blank page and will enable you to examine your thoughts more objectively later on.

Worry as you write

This may sound like odd advice in a book meant to help you compose an essay, but the worrying stage, uncomfortable though it may be, is usually productive. Worrying is thinking.

Plan to rewrite

Don't demand perfection of your prose the first time out. Writing demands rewriting, not only to correct but to beautify. The need for revision does not mean that your first draft is a failure. Writers revise not only to correct errors but to find the smoothest, the most succinct, the most elegant way to say something. Writing without revision is like getting dressed without looking in a mirror.

Allow yourself freedom to experiment

Say something. The essay is your chance to say what you want to say (within the limits of decorum!) the way you want to say it. All that is demanded in an essay assignment is that you think independently (and perhaps with a little help from source material) and write in your own words (perhaps with the occasional quoted expert). Don't allow the fear of criticism to paralyze you at the outset. In your first draft especially, write to suit yourself.

Allow yourself space to write and to make mistakes

Double or triple space. Leave wide margins. Leave one side of the page blank. Use pencil if you like. Or use coloured markers so you can see immediately what is being added or deleted.

Cut and paste literally (or with the aid of a word processor) in order to give yourself the chance to see the complete sequence of ideas.

Develop your own methods of quick notation

As you write, include references immediately after their occurrence in the text. Generally, use the author's last name and a page number in parentheses just after the quotation or the reference in your paper. If you use the documentation suggested by the MLA (see p. 132 of this volume), this notation may be all you need. If not, your notes can be amended later.

If you are using a word processor

If you are lucky enough to be able to compose your essay on a word processor, take advantage of any of its special features that will enable you to write more quickly and more efficiently. Here are some guidelines:

1. Experiment. Take advantage of the speed of the word processor to allow yourself a look at various possibilities in wording and in structure.
2. Write more critically than when you write on paper. Take advantage of the freedom from drudgery offered by the processor to move paragraphs and to revise wording.
3. Learn to proofread from the screen. Better still, doublecheck your proofreading. Check the screen first and then make a hard copy and check it.
4. Don't expect the machine to do everything for you. Even though the mechanical aspects of the essay should be simpler on a word processor, don't fool yourself that careful writing or rigorous revision can be eliminated.
5. Use the time you save by writing on a word processor to think your topic through more carefully, to do more intensive research, and to ferret out every small error.

■ Assembling Evidence

Avoid "tunnel vision"

The success of your essay depends not only on your ability to make your case, but also on the maturity of your critical approach—your fairness, objectivity, and sensitivity to flaws in methodology (yours and others'). Don't let emotions prevent you from assessing the evidence. You may, for example, feel strongly that Canada should provide aid to Third World countries, yet when writing an essay on the subject of development aid, you will have to assess the claims that such aid leads to economic dependency. Objectivity is essential.

Interpret your findings

You cannot expect the citation of a statistic or the inclusion of a quotation to make your point. You must *interpret* the meaning of such evidence. A survey that indicates that 75% of the student population approves of aid to Third World countries does not speak for itself. In order to interpret such findings, you need to know how many people were actually surveyed, whether or not the survey involved a fair random sampling, and whether the questions that made up the survey were clear and unbiased in their wording. Only when you have taken these factors into account can you use the figure to claim, for example, that the student population is, to a large extent, willing to support Third World development.

Avoid "blind spots"

An essay demands that you take a position with regard to the evidence you uncover. That position must, however, be based on objective and unbiased reading of the facts. To ensure that you do not wilfully (or otherwise) misread your evidence, try to formulate both the case for and the case against your position. Include in your essay not only a defence of your thesis, but also arguments that have led you to reject contrary interpretations. For example, if you are arguing that development aid to Third World countries is a humanitarian obligation, you must consider the charge that the resulting private foreign investment is exploitative. You may find that you must concede some points. Such qualification makes your argument all the more objective in its evaluation of the data.

Aim at a better, not an ultimate, theory

When you use evidence to defend your thesis, be realistic in your goals. Your research and your thought together have led you to understand the data in a certain way. Your task is to show that your reading of the material exhibits common sense and attention to recent data. Your theory about the meaning of the evidence should help to explain something. You may find, for instance, that economic dependency only partly explains the continuing problems in the Third World and that internal, national factors play a part as well. Your theory won't be perfect—just the most reliable interpretation of the facts you have found.

■ The Conventional Shape of the Essay

In order to control your material, you must strive to achieve unity within your essay. An essay's unity is the wholeness of the vision, the focus that holds the disparate parts together. Without such wholeness, your essay will seem incomplete or rambling.

To do justice to your assembled arguments and support, the shape of your essay should meet certain of its readers' expectations. To make a good first impression on the reader, your essay should include these basic elements:

1. an *introduction*, moving from general topic to specific thesis, perhaps including a preview of its content;
2. a *body*, developing in turn each of the main points used to support your thesis statement;
3. a *conclusion*, reinforcing and/or summarizing what has been the focus of the essay and suggesting further implications.

Observing these conventional forms will ensure that your essay is clear, pointed, and emphatic from beginning to end.

A good essay possesses a sharp, comprehensive introduction and conclusion, with an expansive body that develops and supports the thesis.

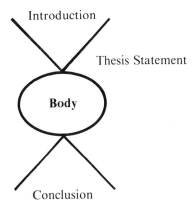

■ Maintaining Unity in the Essay

An essay is a unit: a discussion centred on one basic point. Remember that your essay should focus on your thesis statement. An essay meant to grapple with the causes of the War of 1812 should not discuss its aftermath, just as an essay treating the issue of free will in *Paradise Lost* should find no place for a discussion of epic conventions.

To keep your essay unified:

1. Keep your purpose and basic pattern of argument firmly in mind.
2. Avoid digressions, however interesting, if they cannot be connected to the thesis statement.
3. Avoid padding for the sake of word length. Instead, develop your ideas by referring to the section on patterns of argument and relating them to your proposed thesis statement.

4. Redesign your thesis statement (within the limits of the assignment, of course), if you find your initial focus unappealing or too limited in scope.

Above all, remember the principle of unity:

Everything in an essay should relate directly to the main focus of the paper.

EXERCISE

Read over an essay you wrote recently and note every time you digressed from the main focus of the essay, and every time you added "padding."

Making an Introduction

> It is not generally understood that most writing takes place away from the typewriter. When you finally approach the machine, it is really the beginning of the end.
>
> *Pierre Berton*

Think of your essay, for a moment, as if it were a person. Since an essay will establish some kind of relationship with its readers, the analogy is not altogether far-fetched. Here is some advice on how to proceed after you say "hello."

■ Strike up a Conversation

Obviously, writing a formal essay is more complicated than starting a conversation. But the analogy should provide you with a place to start. How should you begin a conversation? One way is to startle your listener by presenting an exciting piece of information, as a preview of coming attractions. Or, as a recommendation of the value of the work you have done, you can report the words of a well-known, respected authority in relation to your topic. Another method is to pick a fight, by stating the claims, or defining the terms, of the accepted position and then challenging them. Remember that your first task is to convince your audience to pay heed to what you are saying. What all of these tactics have in common is their ability to provoke a response.

Human judgment being the superficial, lazy thing it sometimes is (and professors are by no means exempt), an essay must overcome certain prejudices about its nature. In order to present itself proudly to an instructor, an essay must show immediate signs that it will not be boring, vague, pretentious, or long-winded.

■ Write with Control

Perhaps the most common pitfall among essay writers setting forth the basis of their arguments is long-windedness. Remember that an introduction should be no longer than about one-fifth of the entire essay's length (the best introductions are short and comprehensive—don't go on). If you find that your introduction demands more space than that, you have not narrowed your topic down to a manageable size, or you should be writing a book instead! Never promise in the introduction more than you can deliver in the paper. The first few lines are the best place to limit the scope of your discussion and state the qualifications of your theories. Maintain control of your material, and have some consideration (if not some pity) on your poor beleaguered reader.

■ Write with Conviction

To avoid accusations of boredom, make sure that the introduction shows *how* what you have written matters—to you and to anyone concerned with the subject. Convincing readers that a topic is important is not simply a matter of telling them so; you have to show them, by the tone of your writing, that you are deeply engaged with the topic. Write with conviction, with the feeling that what you are saying will make a difference. Don't negate its value by suggesting that the essay's position is only your opinion. Approach the essay as if it were one side of a lively conversation. Because there is some distance between writer and reader, this interchange is not as immediate as that of conversation, but remember that there is a reader "at the other end of the line." Imagine your reader's responses as you introduce your material, just as you imagine your friend's face as she answers the telephone.

■ Be Conversant

Your introduction is meant to foster an existing knowledge and interest on the part of the reader. Don't tell the reader what he or she already knows. In the case of a literary essay, for example, there is no need to provide a plot summary. Any reader of such an essay should have that material well in hand. In other disciplines, this advice means avoiding the mere recital of material discussed in class, or the careful delineation of a definition that is neither contentious nor germane to what will follow. Write to communicate.

To avoid sounding pretentious, you must use your own voice and your sense of what is appropriate to the occasion. In the introduction, you must lead the reader into your way of thinking. The introduction must make both you and your reader comfortable. To get comfortable with a topic that, three weeks ago, may have been completely unfamiliar to you is part of the task of essay writing. Only when you can *talk* knowledgeably about the subject of your paper are you ready to write about it.

■ Communicate with Your Reader

If carefully designed, your introduction should tell the reader some essential things about you and your work: that you sincerely wish to communicate; that you are conversant with your subject and have convictions about it; that you are confident, in control, and considerate of your reader. All these nouns beginning with "con" or "com" suggest the necessity of forming a relationship *with* someone or something. An introduction with these attributes demands attention and commands respect.

■ Ice-breaking: Tactics for Opening the Essay

If you are at a loss for words when writing your introduction, try one of the strategies in the following list. Suppose, for example, that your essay topic is "Dealing with disagreeable people."

1. **Take the straight and narrow path.** State your thesis bluntly and without preamble. Follow it with a brief statement of the steps in your argument.

   Example

   To deal with disagreeable people, you need a cool head, a blank face, and an icy stare. If you possess these three attributes, you will be guaranteed to outface the opposition and emerge triumphant, even in the most awkward situations.

2. **Try shock treatment.** Give your reader a striking, perhaps shocking example, statistic, or statement to get him or her interested in reading further.

   Example

   How do you deal with disagreeable people? Do you punch them in the nose, trip them as they go downstairs, or threaten to pinch, kick, or bite them? Or, are you more inclined to hurl abuse at them—curse, scream, or mutter invective? While these methods have their advantages—the chief one being that they allow us to vent our rage—such tactics usually fail to get us what we want. Instead of resorting to violence or profanity next time, consider these alternatives: a cool head, a blank face, and an icy stare.

3. **Engage your reader.** Remind the reader that the subject under discussion matters by showing its general importance, before you settle down to your specific line of argument.

   Example

   When I was twelve years old, I tried to return a sweater to a local department store. Naively, I told the woman behind the counter that I wanted a refund because the sweater did not fit properly. She looked at me sceptically. "Why didn't you try it on before you bought it?" she queried. "Because my mother bought it for me," I replied. Was I sounding defensive? Unmoved, she responded, "The sweater was a sale item. There are no refunds on sales items. Sorry, little girl." But she didn't look at all sorry, and I wasn't a little girl. At the time, I was close to tears. Since then, however, I have learned that the best treatment for disagreeable people is a cool head, a blank face, and an icy stare.

EXERCISES

1. Read the following introductory paragraphs and identify the tactic used. Try writing another introduction, using a different tactic:

   a. Men's recreational leagues should not include women. It is important to separate the sexes in such leagues in order to maintain a fair level of competition and to ensure a relaxed atmosphere.

   b. Statistics tell us that suicide is most common among single men and married women. From this information, it would appear that marriage is psychologically healthier for men than for women. A wife, it seems, is an asset; a husband is a liability. Men benefit more than women from marriage because of two things: the nurturing that a wife often provides and the increased status of the married man.

c. Perhaps you know some people who always seem to have lots of time on their hands. They are the ones who go out every Thursday, Friday, and Saturday night. They sleep until 2:00 p.m. every Friday, Saturday and Sunday. They never seem to have any classes, and their homework never gets in the way of having a good time. They watch three hours of television religiously every evening (before they go out). These people, you decide, are amazing. They must put in lots of early morning hours getting reading and assignments out of the way before classes, or else they are geniuses with extensive experience in speed-reading. You are wrong. These people are procrastinators, and with a little bit of determination and effort, you too may join their ranks. Of course, if you are reading this paper in order to avoid doing something of infinitely greater importance, then you won't learn anything new from me.

d. Section 9 of the *Manitoba Human Rights Act (MHR Act)* allows for the implementation of "special programs," more commonly known as "affirmative action" programs. The inclusion of such a section in the *MHR Act* appears to suggest that equality is a goal toward which Manitobans wish to strive, in addition to the elimination of individual discriminatory acts based on the various grounds covered by the *Act*. The purpose of this paper is to consider the intent and underlying assumptions of section 9 and to determine its adequacy as a remedy to systemic discrimination in employment.

2. Analyze the opening paragraph or so of one of your essays. What introductory techniques are used there? Try rewriting the opening to make it stronger.

Drawing a Conclusion

> Great is the art of beginning, but greater the art is of ending.
>
> *Henry Wadsworth Longfellow*

Your concluding paragraph is not only your last word on the subject but also an opportunity for you to reinforce your argument. Listed below are four techniques by which you may reinforce your argument in order to end your paper strongly and convincingly. The essay that builds towards a powerful conclusion will not fade out but will reverberate in the reader's ears.

■ Retrace Your Line of Thought

Retracing does not mean repeating. Since both you and the reader know where you have been, all you need to provide in your conclusion is a reminder of the steps of the journey. You need only to mention key words that have gathered meaning as the argument has proceeded in order for the astute reader (the one for whom you have been writing all along) to "catch your drift." Echo for effect, rather than for reiteration.

To remind the reader of the inherent structure of your essay, make certain to restate the thesis statement in a conclusive manner, and in different words from those which you used in the opening. Doing so will enable you to check to see if the essay has really lived up to your expectations of it. Keep in mind that the essay is meant to be a lively, though formal, conversation. A subtle reminder of the point you have made will aid the readers; a word-for-word repetition will annoy them.

■ Refocus Your Argument

Just as a film director may end a scene by widening the range of the camera or melting into soft focus, so too the essay can take a broader and less stringent view of its subject in its closing.

Widen the focus as you conclude by showing the importance of your topic beyond the immediate concerns of your paper. Beware, however, of writing an overblown conclusion such as "Milton is the world's greatest poet." Instead, include a suggestion for change or perhaps a solution to the problem you have so carefully outlined in the core of the essay.

■ Encourage Response

While the body of your essay requires you to provide answers and to be clear and definite in your thinking and wording, there is *some* room in the conclusion for you to mention tentative ideas, to pose questions, or to offer challenges to the reader. You shouldn't open the floodgates too widely, but it is a good tactic to provoke a response in your reader, provided it is relevant to the topic in question. Beware, though, of starting something you cannot finish, or of introducing a topic that sounds suspiciously like what your essay should have been about.

■ Make Your Words Resound

By the time you reach your conclusion, you should feel that no important argument for your thesis statement has been neglected. This attitude of confidence will allow you to end your paper with a bang rather than a whimper (to invoke, or rather invert, T.S. Eliot). Make sure that the tone conveys a sense of finality, a sense that you have done all that can be expected within the precise bounds of your thesis statement. The conclusion should not, of course, make grand claims that your essay cannot substantiate.

■ Drawing to a Close: Tactics for Ending the Essay

When you come to the end of your paper, consider one of the following ways of formulating a conclusion. Suppose, for instance, that your paper is about the evacuation of Japanese Canadians in World War II.

1. **Decide that enough is enough.** If you find you have nothing pressing to add, say nothing. Don't take this route just because you are tired, though. Make sure that your argument ends on a strong note.

   Example

   Both the federal and B.C. provincial governments acted irresponsibly in rejecting the competent recommendations of the military. The war provided an excuse for those who wanted to cripple the Japanese community. The issue of national security, therefore, remains highly questionable—if not absolutely irrelevant.

2. **Take the wider view.** Examine some of the broader implications of your thesis and the questions it may have raised.

   Example

   Although the evacuation of the Japanese Canadians from the West Coast has been defended as essential to national security, with hindsight it becomes clear that such drastic action was undertaken because of racial prejudice. Japanese Canadians were perceived as a threat to Canada, largely because of their different language, traditions, values, and physical attributes. Their evacuation and internment are a dismal excerpt from Canada's past.

3. **Reinforce your claim.** Remind the reader gently of your line of thought and reiterate your thesis in a slightly different form.

Example

The evacuation and subsequent internment of Japanese Canadians were the result of both long-standing economic and racial conflict, which, already malignant before the war, became the target of bigoted, self-serving politicians who for various reasons were determined to expel these people from Canada.

EXERCISES

1. Read the following conclusions and decide whether they are successful. Why or why not?

    a. For the props department, no two productions are the same. Each play requires adaptation. The prop builder must use his or her knowledge and skills to produce something entirely new and different. Often, the process requires experimenting with new materials or with new tools. The buyer must constantly look for something that may not even exist; it is the prop department's job to find it or to create it. These multiple responsibilities, duties, and challenges make the props department an interesting and diversified place in which to work.

    b. In an effort to become more efficient, manufacturing processes are moving towards computer-integrated technology. Already, European and Japanese companies are using computers in their planning and manufacturing processes. If North American companies do not become automated, they will lose their market share and hurt not only themselves but the North American economy as well. Automation is essential: it will improve the standard of living, ensure a strong position in world markets, and create better jobs. Without it, manufacturing cannot advance.

    c. These examples show that all police officers are not the same: some are truly concerned about the people that they "serve and protect"; some are just putting in time and doing their best to fill a quota; some even have a sense of humour and try to enjoy their work. Whatever their attitude, those I have met were all just doing their job: they caught me breaking the law, and I was punished. I deserved it. Maybe that is why I always say "thank you" when a policeman gives me a ticket.

    d. The Mulroney government has shown itself unable to win the support of the electorate on such issues as free trade, the protection of the environment, and immigration policy. These problems, coupled with the government's inability to lower the deficit substantially, have further eroded support. The prime minister's failure to rally support for his policies will almost certainly take its toll in the popular support of the Conservative party.

2. Analyze the last paragraph of the sample research paper (p. 95). What techniques are used to tie things together there?

3. Analyze the last paragraph or so of one of your previous essays. What techniques did you use to conclude? Can you rewrite these paragraphs to make them more effective?

Writing Paragraphs

> A work of art ... must have a beginning and an end and something of an infinitude between the two.
>
> *Frederick Philip Grove*

Though an essay may not be, strictly speaking, a work of art, it does offer infinite opportunities for the artistic development of your material. What follows are some suggestions on how to develop your paragraphs and how to check to see that paragraphing in the final paper is unified and coherent.

A paragraph must be about one thing. This principle of unity should be so clear that you could compose a heading for each paragraph if the assignment demanded it (and some may).

Logical connections within each paragraph must also be clear. Leaps in logic or unstated assumptions are flaws in your argument that will affect the coherence of the final paper and lose your reader's good will.

Each paragraph is a small step in your total argument, meant to lead the reader onwards through your thought process. Hence, each small part must contribute to the whole pattern. Remember that each small section of your argument, each paragraph, is in fact a miniature model of the essay structure itself.

Each paragraph, like the larger essay, should contain the following elements:

1. a topic sentence that reveals the controlling idea, or thesis
2. support related to the topic sentence
3. unity of focus
4. a smooth transition to the next paragraph

■ The Topic Sentence

A typical paragraph in an essay begins with a topic sentence, a general "umbrella" statement that explains what the rest of the paragraph is about. Anything that does not relate to this controlling idea should be left out.

■ The Support

Your support may take several forms:

1. examples　　　3. connected reasons/definitions
2. statistics　　　4. authorities

Approach the undeveloped arguments in your outline with these four categories in mind. The sources of support will depend on the nature of the assignment: a formal research essay may require all four; a less formal paper will rely chiefly on reasons and examples for its strength.

■ Developing Support for Your Paragraphs

Remember, as you weave your outline into paragraphs, that each discrete unit should contribute something to the illustration of the essay's thesis statement. The paragraphs must argue in defence of the thesis and illustrate its validity.

Some of the following methods are formal adaptations of techniques of argument you may have used before. The list is by no means complete; try to think of other equally effective battle plans.

Present the Facts of the Case. These facts may include statistics used to prove your point. Don't take it for granted that your readers know what you know about the subject.

Example

The good loser is most often the object of considerable admiration; the poor loser is equally often the object of contempt. For example, a recent survey shows that 60% of regular spectators of tennis matches dislike having to watch the temper tantrums of John McEnroe and believe the sport would be improved without such histrionics. To win admiration, one must try to lose gracefully.

Show and Tell. To keep the line of thought going, remember that it is always best to argue by example, rather than by precept. Don't just tell your readers about something. Show them, wherever possible, how your idea works by giving an example.

Example

A good loser must learn to smile genuinely. This smile requires a happy expression showing exactly the right number of teeth: too few teeth will convey insincerity, while too many teeth will make you appear suspiciously predatory.

Establish Connections. Find something in the point you are making which relates to your own experience or to that of your readers. If the essay is formal rather than informal in tone, adapt this advice to show the readers why the subject is important to them.

Example

Yet another aspect of learning how to lose gracefully involves responding to the winner's gestures and comments. The most common gesture is the conciliatory arm-over-the-shoulder motion. This action can be obnoxiously aromatic when it occurs after a high-stress sporting event. The only course of action for losers is to smile bravely, avert their heads when possible, and hold their breath when not. This action is often accompanied by a ridiculous comment such as "I was just lucky" or "it could have gone either way." The latter is especially difficult to deal with when the score was thirty-eight to two! Responding to the comment requires the ever-present smile and some small, sincere comment.

Define Your Terms. If the terminology is clear, don't bother telling your readers what they already know. If, on the other hand, you think that a closer look at a word or phrase that is part of your topic will help your case, draw their attention to it.

Example

After losing a competition, in lieu of a handshake, women are advised to perfect the half-hug and the near-miss kiss. The half-hug consists of lightly placing your hands on your opponent's shoulders, bending your elbows, and appearing to move towards your opponent in a hug-like fashion. This truly is an art, as your bodies must never touch, and you must maintain a minimum distance of two feet. The near-miss kiss is most easily performed during the half-hug. While appearing to move towards your opponent, you place a kiss in the air approximately three inches from her right ear. Although it is not difficult, this procedure does require some practice.

Call in an Expert. Convince your reader by turning to an expert for support. Don't expect readers to take your word for something, if the words of a specialist in the area are available to buttress your own. If the person to whom you refer is a respected authority, your argument will be enhanced.

Example

These suggestions should enable you to maintain your poise in a variety of stressful situations. However, if you are unable to remain calm and have no real desire to gain a reputation as a gracious loser, then may I suggest verbal or physical abuse. It may not be in the interest of good sportsmanship, but I guarantee it will make you feel better! After all, as Knute Rockne said, "Show me a good and gracious loser and I'll show you a failure."

■ Unity

A paragraph, like the essay itself, should have demonstrated the development of your thought by the time your reader finishes it. Each paragraph should lead the reader along in a logical and coherent manner. If your outline has been well planned, the progress of your thinking should be orderly and your conclusion clear. Your paragraphs should each form discrete units, but each paragraph should be clearly connected to what precedes and to what follows.

Example

The Marxist interpretation of history involves certain basic a priori assumptions. It assumes as truth that one's consciousness does not determine one's way of life, but rather that it is the way of life that determines consciousness. It also assumes that the history of mankind can be viewed totally as the history of class warfare. All historical conflict reflects the basic economic conflict between the progressive class which is heralding a new mode of production and the reactionary class which is trying to maintain the old mode of production over which it has control. Because of the importance of conflict in the dialectic, the Marxist maintains that all crucial periods in *history are marked by revolution. Another important assumption made by the Marxist is that the proletariat is the class of the future, since its revolution will usher in the utopia of the classless society. For this reason, Marxist historiography must be on the side of the proletariat; otherwise, it would be reactionary.*

Here the topic sentence is stated at the outset and is followed by an explanation of the Marxists' position. Support is based on the author's reasonable understanding of the tenets of Marxism and their effects on the interpretation of history. The paragraph is a unit because it includes all the *a priori* assumptions to which the student referred in the topic sentence.

■ Pinning the Pieces Together—Transitions

Despite the basic structural independence of the paragraph, the reader must be able to appreciate how it fits into the whole essay. To make the connections clear to the reader, an essay must contain appropriate transitions and linking devices.

Transitions are signals of a turn in thought. They often pose a problem for the novice essay writer simply because our methods of changing or developing the subject in conversation are much less formal and much more spontaneous than in written, rhetorical form.

Ask yourself what your favourite techniques of transition in speech are. Then try to categorize the situations which prompt you to use them. You may find that your list of transitions includes statements like the following: "And you know what else?" to add or elaborate on a point; "You see," to explain in greater detail; "Sure, but," to disagree with another's argument, at the same time conceding to some degree; "What if . . .?" to put forward an hypothesis; "Anyhow," to dismiss the view of your interlocutor; or, "As I said before," to reinforce an earlier point.

Many of these transitions cannot be easily transferred to the printed page. They are too casual to suit the public occasion of the essay. In their stead, the writer must become familiar with and use more formal transitions to enhance the power of his or her rhetoric.

Transitions have many uses. Here are some examples of various transitions:

TO ADD	TO QUALIFY	TO ENUMERATE
and	often	first, second
also	generally	first, next, last
in addition	specifically	
furthermore	usually	
as well		

TO ILLUSTRATE	TO CHANGE DIRECTION	TO SUMMARIZE
for example	but	to conclude
for instance	however	in short
in other words	conversely	finally
that is	although	
	whereas	

TO DRAW A CONCLUSION	TO ESTABLISH CAUSE
hence	because
therefore	for
as a result	
consequently	

Good transitions are like carefully sewn seams. Although not readily notice-able, they are the means by which the garment—your paper—is held together. Shoddy workmanship in your transitions may cause your essay to fall apart.

■ Checking the Overall Pattern of Your Paragraphs

There are two basic tests for the aesthetic appeal of the paragraph.

One of these is to read the first sentence of each paragraph to see if the line of thought is clearly maintained throughout the entire work. That is, do the sentences themselves act as sub-headings to guide the reader through your design? (Note: This test assumes that most paragraphs begin with a topic sentence. Sometimes, however, the topic sentence may appear at the end.)

The other test is to look at the layout of the paragraphs themselves on the printed page. Are they each a manageable length? Do you find yourself not wanting to read them because of sheer typographical intimidation? Do unto your reader as you would have done unto you.

EXERCISES

1. Develop a paragraph using your definition of a term. Compare it with the definition you find in the dictionary as a starting point.

2. Develop a paragraph using a statistic or a quoted authority as support.

3. Write a paragraph establishing a connection or comparison.

4. Develop two paragraphs: one using a real example and one using a hypothetical example.

5. Write two paragraphs: one using a series of small examples to make the same point and one using an extended example to support the same point.

6. Analyze the structure of the following paragraphs. How is unity achieved? What logical connectives or transitions are used?

    a. It's discouraging to discover that although your friends talk big, most of them won't actually do anything about improving things. They won't donate money to the Heritage Foundation, to the Heart Fund, to Foster Parents, or to a political party. Nor will they sponsor a municipal candidate for election into public office. They won't write letters-to-the-editor, or write or call their members of Parliament, ministers, or senators. They won't work to elect good people nor defeat bad ones, nor run for office. They are too busy chasing dollars and golf balls; they don't care enough. Nor should you.

There's probably some kind of ratio that only two out of every 100 are really responsible humans. They carry our burdens, do our dirty work, get criticized by those who won't do the job themselves (I am a critic), and sometimes get assassinated while in office. With these odds, I say, don't expect society to save you: save yourself. No government, no matter how well meaning at the top, is capable of helping you. You are on your own.

b. Joe Cool is a prime example of a "skipper": he arrives at the library by 7:15 p.m., discusses the football game with his friend until 7:35, and finds a carrel on the fourth floor by 7:45. He takes out his books, arranges them neatly beside his writing utensils and calculator, and reads the graffiti on the desk until he falls asleep. At 8:25 a guy from his psych class wakes him up, and they verbally abuse their prof until 8:45. When a pretty young socialite flits by, Joe strikes up a conversation with her, until her six-foot eight, 250-pound boyfriend rescues her. At 9:00, the entire library exits for a break. The true blue skipper will take no less than an hour-long recess; J.C. reluctantly vacates the social area by 10:00 and heads back to the library, stopping to converse with a fellow Argos fan, and poking his head into the games room to see who's there. After going to the washroom, getting a drink of water, sharpening the necessary HB and 2B pencils, and replacing a lead in his eversharp, he settles down to work again by 10:25. At 10:30, the library announcements inform Joe that the circulation desk will close in fifteen minutes; he has to return his two-hour loan material ("How to train a rat to eat") right then. This procedure takes at least ten minutes since the elevators are so slow. On arriving back at his desk at 10:40, he concludes that there is little point in getting down to some serious study now because there are only twenty minutes left before the library closes. So, he packs up his virgin textbooks and leaves, commending himself for having done a good evening's work. He decides to celebrate his new-found intellectual aptitude and heads to the bar for last call.

7. Select paragraphs from essays you wrote in the past. Rewrite any that seem to you to lack a clear topic sentence, unity, or smooth transitions.

Integrating Quotations

To be apt in quotation is a splendid and dangerous gift. Splendid, because it ornaments a man's
speech with other men's jewels; dangerous, for
the same reason.

Robertson Davies

Using a quoted source is like dressing yourself in borrowed finery. For a quoted authority to make its full impression upon your reader, the words must suit the occasion and must be tailored precisely to fit their new wearer—your essay. Rudyard Kipling reports of one bad writer: "He wrapped himself in quotations—as a beggar would enfold himself in the purple of emperors." As clothes do not make the man (or woman), so quotations borrowed incautiously do not make style. A quotation is meant to enhance your argument, not to replace it.

■ Borrow Only What You Need

Remember that quoting is not the only method by which you can support your material. In fact, in disciplines other than English, it is more acceptable to use evidence from a given source without quoting or paraphrasing. In the social sciences, for example, you would generally incorporate pertinent information such as statistics and follow them with a parenthetical reference that acknowledges your source. In these disciplines, the emphasis is on your objective interpretation of the facts.

If, on the other hand, you find that you must refer to a theory or to an explanation of the meaning of some data, the best plan is to paraphrase. Such paraphrasing assumes that the theory being explained is more significant than the words the author used to present it. Since one of the main interests in the social sciences is the accurate reporting of relevant data and of related theories, remember, as you take notes, to paraphrase rather than to quote, taking special care with statistics and their implications.

Borrow words, phrases, and sentences only if they add something essential that you do not already possess. Among these essentials are **credibility**, **power**, and **eloquence**.

(The quotations that follow are taken from Michael Hornyansky's brilliant essay, "Is Your English Destroying Your Image?" in *In the Name of Language!*, Joseph Gold, ed. [Toronto: Macmillan, 1975].)

Credibility

Quote to improve credibility by citing a respected and recognized authority. Or use the quotation as a target for attack, to illustrate that your source should be neither respected nor recognized.

Example

The CBC's news-readers, once modestly reliable (meaning they could be counted on to apologize for errors) have lost their supervisor of broadcast language and now commit cheerfully such barbarisms as "It sounds like he's going to reform."

Power

Quote to demonstrate the power you have at your fingertips, but only to the extent that you will use the quotation. A carefully integrated quotation will show the reader that you have made yourself at home with the sources you have used. Your work will then illustrate your power to cut through trivial details to find the point that demands attention.

Example

Not all change is progress. Some of it has to be resisted, and when possible reversed. If the last ditch needs defending, I'll take my place alongside Samuel Johnson:

> *If the changes we fear be thus irresistible, what remains but to acquiesce with silence, as in the other insurmountable distresses of humanity? It remains that we retard what we cannot repel, that we palliate what we cannot cure.*

(Preface to the Dictionary*)*

Eloquence

Quote rather than paraphrase when no rewording could ever hope to recapture the obvious eloquence of the original writer. Bear in mind that these instances are rare.

Example

[A]s Samuel Johnson observes, "languages are the pedigree of nations."

■ Begging, Borrowing, and Stealing

In order to avoid accusations of theft, a writer, when quoting, must acknowledge a debt to a source. Don't interpret this to mean that you must quote whenever you borrow. When you paraphrase or when you make reference to an idea, you will also admit your indebtedness. Quote only when it is rhetorically the best tactic; that is, when it adds credibility, power, or eloquence.

Technically, you have not stolen an idea as long as you document its original occurrence. But if an idea obviously does not fit your essay, you will reveal to your reader that it is not yours. Such illegitimate borrowing is plagiarism.

Legitimate borrowing takes place when a writer makes sparing use of some source material by fitting it carefully in the body of his or her essay, without altering it or distorting it in a way that would upset the original owner.

Avoid borrowing quotations in such a way that the original meaning is changed or even contradicted. The classic example of this shifty tactic is the movie review cited in an advertisement. It may read, for example, "stunning ... amazing ... not to be believed," when what the reviewer really said was, "A work stunning in its ignorance, amazing in its clumsy handling of the script, and not to be believed when its advertising describes it as the movie of the year."

■ The Fit, Form, and Function of Quotations

The quoted material must fit. It must relate directly to the point under discussion, and it must say something significant. Although quoting often seems like a form of pedantic name dropping, that is not its rightful purpose.

The function of the quotation is usually to illustrate a point that you have already made in your own words. Bringing in an authority on the subject does not, after all, prove anything; it simply shows your awareness of the position of the experts, whether they be on your side or against you.

The form of the quotation is often the most difficult part of essay writing for the novice. Wherever possible, weave borrowed material unobtrusively into the body of your paper, rather than simply tacking it on.

Tacking quotations on

While it may be a relief to stop writing and turn over the responsibility for illustrating your thesis to an authority, proceed with caution. Stopping in the midst of your sentence to introduce someone else (usually with a grand and unnecessary flourish) will diminish your own role as writer.

When you quote, you must remain on the scene, controlling the situation, rather than giving the floor to someone else. Remember, at all times, that the essay is *your* work. When you quote, you do not withdraw completely as if another speaker has been hired to do the job for you.

If you have been in the habit of employing long quotations from your source material, try this experiment with one of your past essays. Read the material through quickly. Do you find yourself skimming over the quoted material, or worse, skipping it altogether? Imagine what effect this kind of reading will have on an essay which depends heavily on outside authorities to make its case.

Weaving quotations in

Wherever possible, make quoted material part of your own sentence structure. This tactic is more difficult but worth the extra effort. First, it will ensure that your reader cannot so easily skip those sections of the paper. Second, it will probably force you to cut quoted material down to the bare essentials, to look at it more closely, and to think of its direct relation to your own thought.

Example

When a mechanic reports that "she's runnin' real good," it takes a pretty stuffy professor to reply that "it is running rather well."

To make this technique work to its fullest advantage, there are some rules to keep in mind.

1. Use an ellipsis (. . .) to indicate words that have been left out. But never use ellipses in a way that misrepresents the original. Ellipses are only permissible when you are making cosmetic changes (such as omitting a connective structure that would not make sense out of context). Keep in mind that you do *not* need ellipses at the start of a quotation, even if you did not begin to quote at the beginning of a sentence, and remember that four dots are used when the omitted words come between two sentences. In other cases, only three dots are necessary.

Example

Hornyansky comments that "in our democratic, colloquial society you are more likely to be censured for using no slang . . . . But of course there are risks in using it too. . . . argot that suits one milieu may draw sneers in another."

The original reads as follows:

I would repeat that in our democratic, colloquial society you are more likely to be censured for using no slang at all. But of course there are risks in using it too. Some sober groups may find your flip ways unacceptable; argot that suits one milieu may draw sneers in another.

2. Use square brackets (even if you have to draw them in in black pen) to indicate words that you have added. Usually you will need these only to indicate small cosmetic changes (such as changing a pronoun to a noun or changing a verb tense to make it consistent with the rest of the verbs in your sentence). Occasionally, you may need square brackets to add a word or two to clarify the context of the quotation.

Example

Hornyansky addresses "third- and fourth-generation Canadians who ... [speak] English (sort of, you know?)."

The original reads as follows:

For I teach third- and fourth-generation Canadians who have spoken English (sort of, you know?) since the crib, yet who have no more sense of English idiom than a recent arrival from the Old Country.

3. When you use a complete sentence to introduce a quotation, follow it with a colon. Otherwise, use a comma or whatever punctuation you would use if the quotation marks were not there.

Example

On the subject of pretentiousness in grammar, Hornyansky remarks, "A question like 'Whom do you mean?' really deserves the answer it gets from Pogo: 'Youm, that's whom.'"

4. Make the terminal punctuation of the quoted material serve your purposes, rather than those of the original. In other words, if the quotation appears at the end of your sentence, close it with a period, even if a comma or other punctuation was used originally.

Example

The original reads as follows:

For he knows that grammar varies inversely as virility; and that if you continue on down to the stadium, you'll find that nobody there plays well.

Your paper will read this way:

Hornyansky believes "grammar varies inversely as virility."

5. Quote exactly. Do *not* distort a quotation, accidentally or deliberately. The first offence is carelessness, the second fraud. If you detect an error of spelling or grammar in the original, you may tell your reader that it is not your mistake by following it immediately with the word [sic] (in brackets as shown). This notation will tell the reader that the fault is not yours.

Example

Hornyansky cites the Hon. John Turner's advertisement "in a British newspaper that his four children 'require a kind and loving nannie [sic].'"

6. Use single quotation marks for a quotation within a quotation, as in the preceding example.
7. Indent passages of prose which are longer than four lines and passages of poetry longer than two lines. When you indent, quotation marks are no longer necessary.

Example

Hornyansky insists on the importance of developing one's own writing style:

> *A man at the mercy of his own style is as comic, and as much to be pitied, as a man at the mercy of drink. Your style ought to express what you are, and you are not the same person on all occasions, in every company. If you seem to be, you are a bore.*

8. When you have gone to the trouble to quote a source, use it. Explain it, remark on its significance, analyze it, do something to show what it contributes to the whole paper. Don't assume its importance is self-evident.
9. Use quotations sparingly. The essay is meant primarily to present *your* views on a given subject.

Elements of Style: Structuring the Sentences

Style is the dress of thought, and a well-dressed thought, like a well-dressed man, appears to great advantage.

Earl of Chesterfield

Variety in your sentence structure will ensure that your reader pays attention, not only to what you say, but also to the way you say it. Try to develop an awareness of the subtle changes in emphasis and reading pace that occur when you modify the structure of a sentence. Such consciousness will enhance your style and impress your reader.

■ Sentence Variation

1. Vary your sentence structure.

The following are examples of different types of sentences:

Simple Sentence—one independent clause

Tracy and Mark engaged in a bout of arm wrestling to settle the restaurant bill.

Compound Sentence—two independent clauses joined by one of the coordinating conjunctions (and, or, nor, for, but, yet, so)

Tracy won the bout, and Mark grudgingly laid a ten-dollar bill on the table.

Complex Sentence—one independent clause joined to one dependent clause

Mark stopped dating Tracy because she was stronger than he was.

Note: Dependent clauses begin with a subordinating conjunction, such as one of the following:

after	because	however	that
although	before	if	though
as	how	since	

Subordinate clauses also begin with words starting with a "wh-"—when, where, why, which, who, while, whereas, what—except where these words introduce questions.

> **Compound-Complex Sentence**—a compound sentence joined to a complex sentence

Dating Tracy was not only hard on Mark's ego, but it was also hard on his pocketbook, since he always found himself paying the bill.

2. **Practise subordination by converting groups of simple sentences you find in your writing into complex sentences.**

Example

The interviewer wondered how the likeable film star could play the part of a villain so convincingly. He explained his method to her. He played the part by imagining himself in his ex-wife's eyes.

Revised

The likeable film star explained to the interviewer that he could play the part of a villain so convincingly because while he acted, he imagined himself in his ex-wife's eyes.

3. **Practise joining simple sentences together using verbal phrases rather than subordinators.**

Example

He didn't know the answer to the question. He decided to invent a plausible lie.

Revised

Not knowing the answer to the question, he decided to invent a plausible lie.

4. **Practise cutting tangled constructions down to size by using simple sentences where the reader might have difficulty in understanding or where you wish to place more emphasis.**

Example

Hate literature is profoundly false and immoral, a violation of a minority's right to dignity and self-respect, and it poses a danger to the group's security by legitimizing attitudes that result in racial violence.

Revised

Hate literature is profoundly false and immoral. It violates a minority's right to dignity and self-respect. It poses a danger to the group's security. It legitimizes attitudes that result in racial violence.

5. **Try converting some of the phrases and dependent clauses in your writing into absolutes (phrases with connecting words removed).**

Example

Because his academic career was destroyed and his dreams of the Nobel Prize for literature were vanquished, he decided to become the best-dressed student in his class.

Revised

His academic career destroyed and his dreams of the Nobel Prize for literature vanquished, he decided to become the best-dressed student in his class.

EXERCISES

1. Join these sentences, using verbal phrases, rather than subordinators.
   a. Cynthia's voice is high-pitched and shrill. It is an asset when she is training her pet bat.
   b. The restaurant patron was in despair at the difficulty of calculating the tip, and finally he gave up.
   c. The heroine found herself in an unfamiliar room. She began to search in a chest of drawers for proof of her dark suspicions about the castle's owner. Finally she discovered a hidden document—a laundry list.

2. Rewrite these sentences using absolutes, rather than dependent clauses.
   a. Even though her examination was a failure, and her essays three weeks late, the student still believed that her work was acceptable.
   b. Edith stormed out of the house, with her head held high.
   c. When he finally lost his patience, he quietly asked his wife for the attorney's telephone number.

3. Rewrite these simple sentences to form complex sentences.
   a. Allen scorns the inanity of sentimental greeting cards. He wears a button to make his disapproval known. It reads: "Have a nice day—elsewhere."
   b. The three of us attended the concert at Stratford. We wanted to sing along. We were delighted. Judy Collins asked the audience to join her on "Amazing Grace."
   c. He was disturbingly eccentric. He kept a snake in the bathtub. She divorced him. He liked the snake better than her.

4. Analyze an essay that you have recently written, or are writing, to determine what sentence patterns you use most commonly. Rewrite some of the sentences and examine the changes in emphasis that such revision creates.

■ Parallelism

Parallelism is one of the basic components of good writing style. The repetitive rhythm of parallel structure allows the reader to anticipate what comes next and to keep the overall construction in mind. Consider the following sentences:

NOT PARALLEL: *She paid for her education by working as a nightclub singer, a waitress, and by borrowing heavily from her parents.*

PARALLEL: *She paid for her education by **working** as a nightclub singer, **waitressing**, and **borrowing** heavily from her parents.*

Making sentences that are logical, powerful, and easy to understand requires a developed sense of parallel construction. To sharpen this sense, you need to become aware of certain basic requirements of balanced sentence structure.

1. Make sure grammatical elements match.

To form a parallel construction, join nouns with nouns, verbs with verbs, participles with participles, adjectives with adjectives, and so on. Connecting words like "and," "or," "but," "yet" are often signals of the need for a parallel construction.

NOT PARALLEL: *The weightlifter was tough, competitive, and he disliked granting interviews to reporters.*

PARALLEL: *The weightlifter was tough, competitive, and unwilling to grant interviews to reporters.*

Since the first two items are adjectives ("tough" and "competitive"), the last item in the series should also be an adjective.

NOT PARALLEL: *People under stress should not expect the use of drugs and alcohol, overeating, or excessive sleeping to solve their problems.*

PARALLEL: *People under stress should not expect drug-taking, drinking, overeating, or excessive sleeping to solve their problems.*

The parallelism is improved when each of the nouns in question has an "ing" form.

NOT PARALLEL: *Manic depression, a form of psychotic behaviour, causes extreme mood changes, the attitudes and activities are radically altered, the sense of reality becomes severely impaired, and relationships are hard to maintain.*

PARALLEL: *Manic depression, a form of psychotic behaviour, causes extreme mood changes, radically alters attitudes and activities, impairs the sense of reality, and jeopardizes relationships.*

The balance is improved by making each of the listed items begin with a verb.

2. Use parallel constructions after "than" or "as."

NOT PARALLEL: *It is better to finish your essay than fail the course.*

PARALLEL: *It is better to finish your essay than to fail the course.*

What follows "than" should be parallel with what precedes. Hence, the word "to" should be repeated.

NOT PARALLEL: *My conclusions are just as valid as the committee.*

PARALLEL: *My conclusions are just as valid as those of the committee.*

The conclusions are being compared, not the conclusions and the committee. Here, the pronoun "those" is used to make the sentence parallel and to avoid the repetition of the word "conclusions."

3. Balance sentence elements connected by correlatives.

Correlatives come in pairs. They include "not only . . . but also," "both . . . and," "either . . . or," "neither . . . nor," "whether . . . or."

The grammatical constructions that follow the first coordinator should also follow the second.

> NOT PARALLEL: *He didn't only apologize to her, but also to her parents, and he got down on his knees on the living room floor.*
> PARALLEL: *Not only did he apologize to her and to her parents, but he also got down on his knees on the living room floor.*

Correlative conjunctions are used here to join a main and a subordinate clause.

> NOT PARALLEL: *Whether it rains or if it snows is a matter of indifference.*
> PARALLEL: *Whether it rains or it snows is a matter of indifference.*

Correlatives are used here to join two main clauses (*it rains* and *it snows*).

Note the revisions in the following sentences:

> NOT PARALLEL: *He kept his promise both verbally and in his actions.*
> PARALLEL: *He kept his promise both in word and in deed.*

What follows "both" should be grammatically parallel to what follows "and."

> NOT PARALLEL: *You either go, or I will.*
> PARALLEL: *Either you go, or I will.*

What follows "either" must be grammatically parallel to what follows "or." In this case, a subject and verb follow both items.

4. Parallel constructions may also be indicated by transitional signposts such as "first," "second," and "third."

> NOT PARALLEL: *The recording star broke his contract: first, ticket sales were slow; second, he was not paid enough; and third, resenting that an animal act had been given top billing.*
> PARALLEL: *The recording star broke his contract: first, because he felt that ticket sales were slow; second, because he believed he was underpaid; and third, because he resented that an animal act had been given top billing.*

5. Make sure that items in a list are grammatically parallel.

> NOT PARALLEL: *This report will deal with four of the attributes of a successful political candidate:*
> *1. experience in political office*
> *2. skill in public speaking*
> *3. ability in dealing with people*
> *4. diplomatic*

PARALLEL: This report will deal with four of the attributes of a successful
political candidate:
1. experience in political office
2. skill in public speaking
3. ability in dealing with people
4. diplomacy

In this case, the items listed have been changed so that they are all nouns; in the incorrect example, the fourth item is an adjective.

Remember that parallel construction need not be confined to words and phrases; it may extend to clauses as well as to sentences. Effective use of parallel structure will enhance your writing by making it clear and balanced.

NOT PARALLEL: All dissatisfied citizens, men or women, young or old, share one
belief: when someone threatens their rights or their needs are not
met, they will be heard.
PARALLEL: All dissatisfied citizens, men or women, young or old, share one
belief: when their rights are threatened, or when their needs are not
met, they will be heard.

"Or" in the corrected sentence joins two subordinate clauses, both in the passive voice.

EXERCISE

Correct any faulty parallelism you find in the following sentences:

1. His diet will be a success if he can do three things: eat less, exercise more, and he'll have to develop an addiction to celery.
2. The job description reads as follows: Applicants require physical strength, sterling good looks, excellent reflexes, a university education, and they must be willing to work for minimum wage.
3. He will make an excellent politician: he is diplomatic, intelligent, a fluent speaker, and he has a face only a cartoonist could love.
4. Donna prided herself not only on being a gifted professor, but among her hobbies included ceramics, windsurfing, and bellydancing.
5. Their wit, charm, and the fact that they have no talent as performers indicate that they would make highly qualified hosts on a talk show.
6. To establish a good working relationship with a foreign client, one must not only learn to speak his language, but also his culture.
7. Ann Landers told her that she should return the towels she had stolen from the hotel and not to steal anything anymore.
8. He was handsome and a shrewd man.
9. Guilt not only nags its victims, but it can keep families together and promote social responsibility.
10. All he really wanted from her was a free meal and a hand to hold.

■ Active and Passive Voice

The voice of a verb tells you whether the subject acts or is acted upon. There are two voices: active and passive. In the active voice, the sentence takes this form:

actor, verb, receiver. In the passive voice, the form is inverted: receiver, verb, actor, and the verb always includes some form of "to be."

In an active sentence, the subject is the actor:

The wildlife photographer tracked the spoor of the lioness.

In a passive sentence, the subject is acted upon:

The spoor of the lioness was tracked by the wildlife photographer.

Keep these points in mind when you decide which voice is more appropriate in a given context:

1. The active voice is more forthright and usually more concise. (The active example above has nine words; the passive sentence has eleven.)
2. The active voice emphasizes the actor; the passive voice emphasizes the receiver of an action. In the example above, the photographer is the subject in the active sample; the spoor of the lioness is the subject in the passive sample.
3. The active voice emphasizes action; the passive is best used to describe stasis.

   ACTIVE: *The chihuahua fastened himself to the intruder's pantleg.*
   PASSIVE: *The chihuahua was fastened to the intruder's pantleg.*

4. The passive voice is awkward when it is used to avoid direct phrasing and results in unclear, lengthy constructions.

   ACTIVE: *Imelda bought one hundred new pairs of shoes last year.* (direct)
   PASSIVE: *One hundred new pairs of shoes were bought last year.* (indirect: easy to omit the name of the person who bought them and thus to avoid holding someone responsible)

   ACTIVE: *Every morning, Betty Lou consulted her horoscope in the newspaper.* (clear)
   PASSIVE: *Every morning, the horoscope in the newspaper was consulted by Betty Lou.* (unclear)

5. The passive voice is occasionally useful to avoid overuse of the pronoun "I." Be wary of overusing the passive voice, however.

   ACTIVE: *I am basing this report on actual interviews with eye witnesses.*
   PASSIVE: *This report is based on actual interviews with eye witnesses.*

6. Remember that the passive voice is useful when you wish to emphasize the receiver of the action, rather than the performer.

   ACTIVE: *People could hear the explosion for miles.*
   PASSIVE: *The explosion could be heard for miles.*

Since it is unimportant who heard the explosion, the passive is preferable here.

7. The passive voice is also the best choice when you wish to avoid being too personal.

ACTIVE: *You must pay the bill by next week.*
PASSIVE: *The bill must be paid by next week.*

Since the notice of the bill is meant to be formal and impersonal, the passive is preferable here.

EXERCISE

Where appropriate, rewrite these sentences by changing them from passive to active or from active to passive. Some may be fine as they are.

1. On her birthday, Carrie was taken by her boyfriend to see *Cats.*
2. The screenwriter of the horror movie was accused by the acerbic movie critic of having all his taste in his mouth.
3. *The Moons of Jupiter* was written by Alice Munro.
4. The ashtray was made in a ceramics course by Marge that perched on the mantelpiece.
5. Attention must be paid by the powers that be if they are not to become the powers that used to be.
6. People evacuated the department store after the bomb threat.
7. The picnic feast was eaten by the shivering tourists in the pavilion, surrounded by unruly children from a nearby summer camp.
8. The dinner was planned by the host to serve only a vegetarian menu.
9. Students will write examinations in April.
10. The tap dance was performed by Arthur as part of the entertainment at the wedding.

Setting Tone

Take the tone of the company that you are in.
Earl of Chesterfield

Tone is one of the most elusive features of a writing style, whether your own or someone else's. The tone of your essay writing, if it is to avoid clashing with the reader's expectations, should be neither too loud nor too soft. Harsh tones may antagonize your readers. Conversely, gentle tones may make your arguments seem too weak or too bland.

Tone in writing may be compared to tone of voice. What follows will show both which tones to avoid and which to emulate. When you read your paper aloud to check for errors, listen for potential problems.

The tone you choose must fit the purposes of your essay. If the assignment is a formal research paper, the tone must be appropriately formal as well. If, on the other hand, you are writing an informal, more personal paper, your tone may be correspondingly more casual. The expectations of your readers—"the company that you are in"—define the tone for you.

■ Tones to Avoid

Avoid whispering

A tone that is too "soft" suggests that the writer is unsure of the words and the thoughts behind them. Words that are too tentative, too hesitant, are one sign of a whispering tone. Phrases like "it seems to be" or "perhaps" or "it could be that" are indications of the problem. Another signal is the overuse of qualifying phrases such as "however" and "to some extent." Although some qualifications are a good idea, too many may cause the reader to doubt your confidence in your own position.

Avoid chatting

A chatty essay is most often the result of incomplete planning and outlining. If your paragraphs or your sentences seem to trail off or to lead to unexpected conclusions, if your ideas seem linked by random association, if your language seems too colloquial or offhand, and if you treat the reader as a chum rather than as an interested observer, you may be accused of chattiness. The cure for chattiness is care, revision, and a polite, though distanced, regard for the readers.

Avoid emotiveness

An emotive tone is struck when a writer attempts to describe his or her feelings in a high-flown, exaggerated way. Often, what results sounds falsely sentimental or hackneyed. Such a tone is often found in introductions and conclusions, particularly when a writer tries to wax poetic about his or her opinions. Although opinions are warranted in an essay, it is nevertheless not necessary to praise Shakespeare as a great playwright at the end of a paper analyzing the structure of *Macbeth*, nor to tell the reader that nuclear disarmament is a matter of life and death for the human race. Show your feelings by supporting your opinions; don't just declare them.

Avoid declaiming

Treat your reader as an equal. Though you may well be teaching, your role is to reason with your reader and to assume his or her rationality. Any style that repeats points too much, or goes on too long, or explains more than the reader needs, is declaiming. This tactic, in combination with a pretentious vocabulary, is disastrous. When you revise, check to see that your writing is transparent, that it does not need to be deciphered to be understood. Avoid words that intimidate the reader because of their length or their obscurity. Choose instead the word that will most clearly express your meaning. Check also to see that the essay is within the required word limit.

In a formal essay, it is also wise to limit the use of rhetorical questions, or to avoid them altogether. Your job is to tell the reader something, not to ask questions.

Avoid shouting

Make sure that your essay does not inadvertently antagonize its readers. It may be your job to defend your viewpoint, but you must not assume that your readers are opponents. This problem with tone is especially prevalent in essays that attempt to refute someone else's position. In these cases, the force should be in the logic of your argument, rather than in the tone of your voice.

Use personal pronouns with discretion

Avoid directly addressing your reader in formal essays. "You" and "your" may alienate the readers if your assumptions about their knowledge or their attitudes are incorrect. It may even sound cheeky or overbearing. If you can, keep the readers on your side; if you know they disagree, keep them at a formal distance.

A research or formal expository essay also may demand that you avoid the use of "I" in writing. If you are forbidden the use of "I" by an instructor, respect that condition.

Do, however, try to avoid awkward impersonal constructions and self-conscious references. Never refer to yourself as "the writer" or "the author."

On the other hand, if "I" is acceptable, *use* it. Your relationship to your reader in a formal essay is meant to be a professional one, but that does not mean that personality has no place, simply that you must know its place, and respect the polite distance imposed between you and the reader.

Example

> X *It is the opinion of this writer that* ... (too stuffy)
> X *In my opinion* ... (too weakly subjective)
>
> ✔ *This paper contends that* ...
> ✔ *I will show that* ...

■ Tones to Emulate

Modulate your writing style

A modulated voice is controlled. Despite the moods of the writer, it shows restraint, politeness, and judgment. Your tones in private conversation may be more varied; in the essay, however (except in the freer personal essay), your tone should be cool, professional, unruffled, and firm.

Imitate the best

Read the essays in newspaper editorials and news magazines, as well your fellow students' work. Textbooks and critical material may also serve as examples, though you must choose with discretion. And listen. The tone of classroom lectures is often a good index of what is expected in a paper.

EXERCISE

Assume the role suggested and write a response for each of the following situations.

YOUR ROLE	THE AUDIENCE	THE SITUATION
suspected criminal	jury mother policeman cohort	explaining your whereabouts on the night of the crime (assuming that you are guilty)
unfaithful spouse	partner lawyer children	explaining your failure to come home
angry customer	salesperson manager friend	returning some defective merchandise
child	mother aging relative sibling	receiving something you don't like as a gift
party-goer	host or hostess escort	leaving an unsuccessful party
student	instructor fellow student parents	complaining about a low grade

PART FOUR

Writing the Essay

The Case for Native Self-Government in Canada:
An Argument

Janice Pelletier
Politics 210
Professor Erskine

SOURCES TO CHECK:
- CANADIAN PERIODICAL INDEX
- CANADIAN NEWS INDEX
- THE CANADIAN ENCYCLOPEDIA

Role Playing

> The essayist . . . can pull on any sort of shirt, be any sort of person, according to his mood or his subject matter.
>
> *E. B. White*

Role playing is a vital part of the skill of essay writing. You must write the essay confident of your role as an expert. In this chapter, we will modify the general principles of essay writing according to the various purposes of different types of essays, and describe a role you might adopt as the author of one of these types. In addition, the chapter emphasizes the kind of reader or audience that each of the different essay types has. All of the types described share the general characteristics that we have already discussed:

1. a narrow thesis statement
2. a clear outline
3. carefully delineated patterns of argument
4. a unified structure—introduction, body, and conclusion
5. a coherent approach to the integration of support materials
6. an attention to sentence structure, emphasis, and tone

Remember that many of the steps involved in writing the different types of essays described in this chapter overlap. But whether an essay is meant as an informal discussion or as a formal research paper, the steps outlined above are essential. No less important are the steps in revision described in Chapter 17.

This chapter will show you how to prepare yourself for certain specialized types of essay writing. Consult it for advice geared to the particular task at hand.

■ The Expository Essay—Essay as Teacher

> The true education is not to give a man a standard of living, but a standard of life.
>
> *Gratton O'Leary*

The expository essay is the most common essay assignment. It is based on the premise that you learn best about something by trying to teach it to someone else. In other words, the expository essay asks you to play the role of teacher, by presenting your chosen material according to your sense of its meaning and structure.

The expository essay exposes: it shows your approach to a particular subject. As in all essay writing, you must develop a general topic into a specific thesis statement, you must prepare an outline, and you must determine the patterns of argument appropriate to your discussion. The expository essay is different only because its object is primarily to *teach*, rather than to persuade, to present research material, to review, or to express personal conviction.

There are four stages involved in writing the expository essay:

1. Finding your focus
2. Planning your structure
3. Adjusting your level of language
4. Testing your results

These stages, while much the same as those outlined in the sections on developing, designing, and drafting the basic essay, are all affected by your role as teacher, and hence they need special consideration.

■ The Role of the Expository Essay

Before you begin, try to see your task in terms of its audience and its purpose.

AUDIENCE: a curious, but uninformed reader, whom you address in a professional but approachable way

PURPOSE: to present some important idea in a way that clarifies it, shows your attitude toward it, and answers questions the reader might have

With these criteria in mind, you can now adjust the stages in writing to suit the occasion.

Finding your focus

1. Find a subject that you know something about and are genuinely interested in, if possible.
2. Establish your objectives. Like a teacher, you should know what you want your reader to learn from your work.
3. Limit your subject to what can be thoroughly explained within the word length of the assignment. What you propose to show or explain is, in this case, your thesis statement.

Example
___

Subject: Sheep shearing
Objective: To show how it is done
Limitation: One technique, explained step by step

Body: How to shear a sheep
- holding sheep
- shaving from left to right
- shaving underside
- shaving from right to left
- shaving neck
- picking up fleece
- rolling fleece and tying it

Other tasks done at sheep-shearing time
- clipping hooves
- worming
- tagging ears
- checking health of sheep

Conclusion: Qualities needed in a sheep shearer
— all those listed in the introduction (as well as a sense of humour)

Connection of Ideas: Check to see that ideas in the outline are properly categorized, in the right order, and parallel in grammatical structure.

Planning your structure

1. Break down the parts of your subject clearly in an outline.
2. Choose the pattern(s) of argument that will allow you to explain most clearly.
3. Connect the steps in your thought logically and clearly.

Example

Thesis statement: "To shear a sheep properly, one must be aware of the following essential steps in the process."

Pattern of argument: Process: how to shear a sheep
Breakdown of ideas: Rough outline
Introduction: Qualities needed in a sheep shearer
- industry
- strong back
- speed
- experience and knowledge

Adjusting your level of language

1. Keep your reader's level of knowledge in mind.
2. Define all terms likely to be unfamiliar to the reader.
3. Make language concrete, concise, and clear.

Example

Level of knowledge: Explain what tools are used to shear the sheep, rather than leaving the process to your reader's imagination.
Use of terms: Use words like "sheep" rather than "ruminant animals of the genus *Ovis*."
Concrete, concise, clear language: Tell what the shearer does rather than explaining what shearing is in the abstract.

There is no wool on the front legs, so the shearer must lean over the animal to shave its hind leg. With one hand, the shearer presses the hind leg joint forcing the sheep's leg to straighten, so that it is more easily shaved.

Testing your results

1. Check your work to see that it is as clear as possible. Put yourself in your reader's place: would you learn from the essay?
2. Have someone else read your work to see that it is readily understandable.
3. Proofread carefully to see that your writing does justice to your thoughts.

Example

Check to see that the relative positions of sheep and shearer are clear at all times.

> *The sheep is then flipped onto its other side, and the shearer finishes shaving its neck. When the wool is flipped back, the shearer lays the sheep down and holds it down by placing one shin on the animal's neck.*

■ The Persuasive Essay—Essay as Lawyer

> He who only knows his side of the case knows little of that.
>
> *John Stuart Mill*

The persuasive essay aims at convincing the reader of the truth and validity of your position. Its subject matter is controversial, its thesis one view of the issue. Your task is to win your reader over with your credibility, your wealth of support, and your good reasoning.

Unlike the expository essay, which simply aims to *show* the reader something, the persuasive essay, by taking one side of a controversial issue, aims to *convince* the reader.

Prepare the persuasive essay according to the following stages:

1. Study the issues
2. Pick a side—your thesis statement
3. Make a case for the defence—your support
4. Consider opposing viewpoints, and qualify or refute accordingly
5. Test your argument for fairness and effectiveness
6. Direct your argument, first in outline, then in final form

A persuasive essay may or may not demand that you engage in extensive research to support your case. It does, however, demand that you keep your writing role in mind.

■ The Role of the Persuasive Essay

Tailor your essay to fit its special demands.

AUDIENCE: readers who have not made their minds up about a controversial matter and who are willing to make a fair and impartial judgment

PURPOSE: to convince them that your informed opinion on a particular subject is the best one

With these points in mind, consider the stages of the persuasive essay. Suppose you are writing a philosophy paper on the issue of capital punishment. Research is not a major requirement; what is required is your independent, well-formulated viewpoint toward this controversial subject.

Study the issues

Before you take sides, you must examine all the angles of the question. Make a list of pros and cons about any issue that must be decided or question that must be settled.

Example

Issue: Capital punishment: on what philosophical grounds is it justified, if any?

PROS	CONS
- protects society	- is subject to error
- is expedient	- is inhumane
- acts as a deterrent	- improves nothing

Pick a side

1. Choose the side for which you can muster the most support. If possible, choose a thesis that you genuinely believe in.
2. Define your position by making a claim or by arguing against another's claim.

Example

Side chosen: Capital punishment is not justifiable.
Position defined: Capital punishment is not justifiable because
    1. it is subject to error;
    2. its use is needlessly cruel according to the Constitution;
    3. its deterrent value is no more effective than a life sentence;
    4. it is based on retribution rather than on the need for society's protection; and
    5. it is final.

Make a case for the defence

1. Gather support for your arguments. In some instances, this support will come from books or journals, though it may also come from your own clear understanding of the issue.

2. Use your own good reasons, and if research is required, use statistics and expert opinion as further support.

Example

(Reasons)

Capital punishment should be abolished because it is based on sheer retribution. It argues that a person "deserves" to be killed for the crime of killing someone else. From a utilitarian perspective, the idea of retribution is immoral, because it is not really conducive to anyone's happiness, and it, in fact, causes suffering. Since no benefits are gained from a criminal's death, some other method, involving less pain for the criminal and his or her family, would be just as effective.

Example

(Statistics)

An argument used to support the return of the death penalty in Canada is that the threat of death as punishment for a murder will act as a deterrent. If the death penalty did act as a deterrent, the number of homicides in Canada would have increased since 1976 when capital punishment was abolished. Since 1976, however, the number of homicides in proportion to the population has not changed. Therefore, the argument that the death penalty acts as a deterrent is invalid.

Example

(Expert opinion)

Section 7 of the Canadian Constitution Act, 1982, states, "Everyone has the right to life, liberty and security of the person and the right not to be deprived thereof except in accordance with the principles of fundamental justice." Section 12 of the Act states, "Everyone has the right not to be subjected to any cruel and unusual treatment or punishment." The reinstatement of the death penalty would grant the state the right to kill without sufficient justification, since it cannot be proven that capital punishment is a more effective deterrent than prison. The return of the death penalty would thus needlessly perpetuate a cycle of violence in contradiction to the principles of the Constitution.

Consider opposing viewpoints

1. Anticipate objections to your arguments as you go along.
2. Treat the opposition fairly.

Example

Anticipated argument: Capital punishment guarantees protection.
Fair treatment: some acceptance of the truth of the objection

It may be argued that capital punishment would guarantee society's protection from convicted murderers. Although that statement is true, it must be pointed out that society is generally well protected by the system of imprisonment already in force. It might also be argued that capital punishment would protect society from the insane as well, but that does not mean that it is morally right to kill those judged insane. The idea of social protection, then, is not sufficient to warrant the use of capital punishment as opposed to imprisonment.

This argument draws an analogy between the treatment of convicted murderers and that of the insane.

Test your argument for fairness and effectiveness

1. Check for flaws in the argument.
2. Weigh your words carefully, avoiding obviously biased or vague, unconsidered words.

Example

> *Capital punishment should be abolished because anyone knowingly willing to risk the death penalty must be insane, and those who do not know what they are doing are not responsible for their actions.*

Checking for flaws: Try to simplify the statement to see the line of argument and its logical consequences.

FIRST PREMISE: Anyone who risks death is insane.

SECOND PREMISE: It is immoral to hold insane people responsible for their conduct.

CONCLUSION: Therefore, capital punishment is immoral and unjust, and it should be abolished.

There is a flaw in this argument. The assumption that persons who commit murder under threat of capital punishment are insane because they willingly risk the punishment of death makes any debate for or against the efficacy or morality of the death penalty spurious. The insanity argument *a priori* effectively *denies* capital punishment on any grounds whatsoever.

The argument does not hold up logically, because of a weakness in the first premise. Hence, it cannot be used as support for the thesis statement.

Weighing your words: It is important to define terms like "insanity" with scrupulous fairness if the case is to be strongly supported. In the argument above, the definition of insanity is so broad that it would include *anyone* who might risk his or her life—even if it were to save someone else's.

Direct your argument

1. Remind your readers of the points you are making by reinforcing them as you go along.
2. Engage your readers as comrades-in-arms, not as antagonists. Assume that they are reasonable, and open-minded about the issue. Do not assume antagonism on their part.

Example

Look at these techniques in the following paragraphs concluding the paper on capital punishment:

There remains one argument for the abolition of capital punishment that is difficult to refute: its finality. As long as our system of justice remains capable of error, it would be presumptuous of us to enforce capital punishment unless it has some special deterrent effect which has not been revealed by this evidence.

From the evidence examined, then, there are no special reasons to support capital punishment.

Reinforcement: Strongest point last: finality

Reader engagement: Use of "us" and "our" (though, since this wording is not always permissible in a formal paper, check with your instructor)

■ The Essay Examination—Essay as Athlete

> All good writing is swimming under water and holding your breath.
>
> *F. Scott Fitzgerald*

Essay examinations are frequently a source of panic because they strip the writer down to the bare essentials. Without hours of preparation to cover your flaws, whether in knowledge or fluency, you may feel exposed—unless your work is genuinely in good shape.

A prepared formal essay wears its style as you would wear a suit. An essay examination, because of its time limitations, is brief but not without style. Writing an essay exam is like wearing a bathing suit. Its impact depends on the shape you're in.

The advice that follows will help you write a better examination, if you approach it in stages:

1. Getting in shape
2. Coping with exam shyness
3. Making the material fit
4. Taking the plunge
5. Standing out in a crowd

■ The Role of the Essay Examination

Remember your reader and your aim:

AUDIENCE: an expert (not an antagonist) who wishes to test your knowledge and facility in his or her discipline

PURPOSE: to show what you have learned and how you can apply it

Getting in shape

An examination is only the product. What determines its outcome is your preparation, not only in the nervous hours immediately before it, but in the days and weeks preceding it as well.

To make your performance on the exam easier and more predictable, prepare for it gradually. If you have faced your fears throughout the year, the final countdown should not be anxiety-ridden. At least, your conscience will be clear if you have attended class, read the textbooks, and completed the course work.

Coping with exam shyness

Analyze the shape you're in

Be brave. Take a good hard look at yourself. Judge your past performance in the course. Consider the amount of work you have done. If you're already in good shape, this step will increase your confidence. If not, read on.

Limber up

Even a well-prepared student will need to warm up for the examination by conducting a review. Review course work by setting up a reasonable work schedule and then follow it (with some flexibility, of course).

Review does not mean reread. Review should be refreshing, just as a warm-up exercise is meant to get you ready for more and not to drain you of energy. Review is just part of the routine. Look through your notes and your texts, as well as your past essays and tests. This process will be easier if you have highlighted important points beforehand (and if you have done all the required work in the first place).

Locate problem areas

To overcome shyness about the exam, you must confront your fears. Ask yourself, unflinchingly, what are you afraid of? If you find that you are worried about some specific problems in your understanding of the course, pay particular attention to these. The benefits will be twofold: you will conquer some of your fear, and you will learn something.

Making the material fit

In order to learn anything, you must make it a part of yourself. You must carry it away with you and get carried away with it (while still keeping your feet on the ground).

To gain full possession of the course material, you will use **memory**, **fluency**, **application**, and **imagination**. Here's how.

Memory

There is no learning without memory, though memory is just the first step in turning course material into something of your own. To sharpen your skills of recall, try reading aloud, so that both sight and hearing can register the information.

Concentrate on facts and significant details. Help your memory along by making associations, or by visualizing material. These tactics will trigger memory when you're stuck for words.

If memorizing is not your strong point, don't despair. Although an essay exam demands that you have some facts at your fingertips, how the facts are presented, how they are used, and what you create out of them are equally important.

Fluency

To make yourself an expert in a discipline, learn how to speak its language as you master its content. Make the terms a part of your language, by learning to define them, by including them in speech, and by using them in writing. When imagining how you would answer a question, talk to yourself. Jot down notes. The more conversant you are with specialized language in your subject area, the more gracefully you will write under pressure.

Application

Make sure you can use what you know. To apply your knowledge, you need to supply a context. Don't just repeat the facts: question the material. As you review, note questions that the textbook may have raised. Keep in mind any questions raised in class or topics distributed for review that strike you as pertinent. These may prove useful come exam time.

Imagination

All work and no play would make a dull examination and certainly a grim study period. Approach the test and its preparation with a sense of play, if at all possible. Wonder about its potential. Don't confine your imagination to the tried and true; experiment with some ideas of your own. Develop a theory or two, as if you were preparing for a formal essay. You may well get a chance to try them out on the examination. The difference between an A and a B is often a desire to develop your own ideas and to create something new out of the material.

Taking the plunge

Writing an examination successfully depends on two factors: what you know *and* what you can say about it in a limited time. To make the best use of your time, follow this basic pattern: **read, sketch, write, skim.**

Read the questions carefully

Before you get your feet wet, so to speak, read over the entire exam. Take careful note of the instructions. If you are given a choice of questions, devote a few minutes to their selection. Allot an appropriate amount of time for each question and *adhere to that schedule*. It is wise to begin with the questions you know best.

Look for questions to challenge you. Remember that an essay question does not necessarily have a correct answer. An essay simply tries, as its name suggests, to come to terms with a provocative, perhaps troubling question.

Become familiar with these common examination terms:

Explain

If you are asked to *explain*, be thorough in your approach and ready to clarify in detail, as though you were teaching the reader. Both structure and substance are needed, so be prepared to show both breadth and depth in your treatment of the question.

Example

The federal Progressive Conservative Party has been called the "normal opposition party." Explain. What must the federal Progressive Conservative Party do to become the "normal government party"?

Begin by using facts to explain the label of "normal opposition party." These facts should be available to you from the course material. Then, making sure to refer to appropriate sources, discuss various theories of what is needed to ensure Conservative success at the polls.

Discuss

If asked to *discuss*, use the latitude of the question to focus on some part of the problem that captures your attention and allows you to present a lively, informative, and thoughtful consideration of the problem. Treat the question as if you were writing a less than formal essay—as indeed you are.

Example

Discuss the ways in which family ties and loyalties dramatically expand the inner conflicts and crises of conscience in **Huckleberry Finn** *and* **King Lear**.

Begin by focusing on the conventional bond between parents and children. Show how the bonds are broken in both works. Then you could go on to show how a new sense of family is created for both Lear and Huck, in the levelling process that occurs in both works. Remember to include many examples to support your points.

Outline

If asked to *outline*, put your emphasis on the bare bones of the argument—the facts—rather than on the flesh. An outline will require you to place more stress on the shape and the sequence of your subject, rather than the substance.

Example

Outline how and why geographical factors are so strongly evident in classical mythology.

Your outline should be broadly based, isolating a number of examples of geographical factors in a variety of myths, rather than in one or two. Follow these examples with a discussion suggesting some of the reasons for this phenomenon. Aim at broad coverage rather than deep analysis.

Compare and Contrast

If asked to *compare and contrast*, or simply to *compare*, remember that the object is to show the relationship between two things. Focus the essay on the connections and differences you find by setting two things side by side in your sketch.

Example

Compare and contrast the women's movement of the late nineteenth and early twentieth centuries with the women's movement which began in the late 1960s.

Begin by making an outline to discover the main similarities and differences. Say, for example, that the main similarities include the desire to change attitudes toward working women and the desire to gain more influence in the workplace. The differences might include the earlier movement's focus on political rights and the later movement's focus on issues relating to sexual harassment on the job. You could compare and contrast not only the goals of the movements, but also the relative success of each of them. Then you need a summary of your findings, in order to compare these two movements more generally.

Sketch

Sketch out your answers to the questions chosen. First, let yourself go. Jot things down helter-skelter as they occur to you. Then, try to gather material into categories for discussion. Avoid getting embroiled in outlines too complex or too demanding for the time allowed.

Sketch your answers in the briefest possible form. As you do so, use key words in the question to guide your responses. Above all, obey the terms of the question as you work in the things you want to say.

Write

Sketching your material enabled you to get warmed up. Therefore, the writing process itself should be more graceful and more organized. To ensure an organized presentation, fall back on established essay writing habits. Begin at the beginning. Make sure your answer has an introduction, a body, and a conclusion. While these sections will be hastier and less polished, do not abandon structure entirely.

The main thing to keep in mind is the connections you are making between the question and the knowledge you brought with you into the exam. Refer to your sketch and to the original question as you write, but also allow yourself the freedom of an unexpected idea or a unique turn of phrase, as long as it doesn't interfere with the basic flow of your answer.

Let the words flow, but keep the writing legible. Write on every other line as a courtesy to your reader.

Skim

Force yourself to read your answers quickly and to make small changes. To neglect this stage is to force your instructor to become the proofreader—a proofreader who might become annoyed at your carelessness. A small mistake is forgivable; reckless abandon is not.

Standing out in a crowd

Now that you know how to pass an essay examination, you may well wonder how to surpass expectations. Though you are writing the examination along with perhaps hundreds of other students, there are ways of making your exam style unique without defying the conventions of test writing.

What does a bleary-eyed instructor, marking two hundred essay questions, look for in an answer?

Definition

An essay examination is your chance to show your understanding of how some terminology in the subject area works. Unlike a multiple-choice exam, this kind of test will allow you to use the language of the discipline precisely and fluently.

Direction

Your answers should be pointed directly at the questions. Don't make the mistake of trying to say everything; you can't assume that the instructor will give you credit if he or she can find the right answer somewhere in your paper. You also can't assume that your instructor will want to look for your answer. Make your answer easy to find.

Detail

While even an exceptional student cannot remember all of the fine points in a complex body of work, it is certainly possible to learn a smattering of appropriate details on a variety of subjects. Such details may be inserted, where applicable, as you are writing the exam. Details have the effect of a close-up. They allow you to focus on something precise, and they reveal your careful reading of your subject matter.

Depth

To demonstrate depth of knowledge, an examination must show that the writer has thought about the implications of the subject and of the specific question. Dive in. Don't avoid entirely the deeper complexities of a question in favour of its superficial requirements. Where possible, do more than you need to do. Answer questions seriously; you are writing as a curious and concerned expert. Address your subject, not as an illustration of how well you have learned it, but rather as a serious attempt to advance the subject matter itself.

Discovery

A brilliant exam will show what a student has learned above and beyond what the instructor has taught. If you have some insight or even some questions about the material which have not been raised in class, this is your opportunity to voice them. Never recite the answer to a question based on your memory of a lecture unless you have, sadly, nothing of your own to add to the material. An exam should occasionally allow you to take intelligent, calculated risks.

■ The Informal Essay—Essay as Friend

> We reproach people for talking about themselves, but it is the subject they treat best.
> *Anatole France*

In most cases, the essays you write as part of your course work will be formal in tone. When you are allowed the luxury of writing an informal essay, follow these basic suggestions:

1. Be yourself
2. Choose a comfortable subject
3. Experiment with style and subject
4. Shop around

■ The Role of the Informal Essay

The informal essay affords you greater freedom and a more casual approach than the formal essay. Although the same writing process is demanded in the informal essay—it too needs a thesis statement, a typical essay shape, and a command of the mechanics of writing—what you say and how you say it are a matter of invention rather than convention.

AUDIENCE: friendly company who find your perspective stimulating

PURPOSE: to talk about anything that appeals to your imagination

Be yourself

The informal essay should let the reader learn about you and about your subject. Whereas you are obliged to keep a restrained and professional distance in the formal essay, you should maintain a casual and personal tone in the informal essay. Someone reading your paper will learn not only the facts and figures of your subject, but also some of your characteristics and your attitudes.

You will necessarily be more exposed: flaws in your arguments, biases in your attitudes, and unattractive aspects of your personality may show. The informal essay is by definition a face-to-face meeting between you and the reader. To prevent excessive vulnerability, you must examine your attitudes scrupulously, and be prepared to face your reader's reaction—alone.

Choose a comfortable subject

Whereas a formal essay must be logical, objective, tight, and well supported, an informal essay allows you to be more subjective in your viewpoint, more personal in your selection of supporting material, and more idiosyncratic in your approach.

The formal essay may argue a life-and-death matter; the informal essay is, by contrast, an intellectual exercise for its own sake. This characterization does not mean that the informal essay cannot be heartfelt or deeply important—but its tone is less public, its argument closer to your personal interests, and its value less dependent on knowledge of facts than it is on grace and eloquence.

Experiment with subject and style

You must draw the material and the viewpoint from your own sense of the subject, rather than looking to authorities for defence.

In an informal essay, your object is to keep your reader interested in what you have to say. You cannot assume that the subject is intrinsically appealing to the reader from a professional standpoint, as you do in the formal essay. Since the material you choose in the informal essay reflects you and your personal understanding of the matter, you must appeal to your reader personally and share your opinions enthusiastically.

The informal essay allows you the opportunity to experiment with language in a way that would not be appropriate in a formal or research essay. Try writing as you speak—without lapsing into grammatical and structural errors. For example, in an informal essay, you can use contractions (don't, can't, etc.) which are generally not acceptable in a formal essay.

Shop around

Make an effort to read some personal essays, whether in newspaper editorials, magazines, or the "collected works" of a classmate. Here are some choices for stylistic study:

Woody Allen	Allan Fotheringham
Harry Bruce	Joey Slinger
Michele Landsberg	Lewis Thomas
Russell Baker	Ray Guy
Fran Lebowitz	James Thurber

■ The Literary Essay—Essay as Analyst

Literature is news that *stays* news.

Ezra Pound

The literary essay requires you to read, to analyze, and to come to terms with the meaning of a piece of literature. Whether it demands secondary sources or simply focuses on the literary work itself, the literary essay demands that you show your understanding of how and why the work is put together the way it is.

Write the literary essay according to the following stages:

1. Formulate a thesis about the work
2. Read the work closely
3. Use secondary sources
4. Select only the best supporting evidence
5. Quote often, but not at great length
6. Write in the present tense
7. Write with both the text and the argument in mind
8. Revise with style

AUDIENCE: someone who has read the novel, or poem, or short story, but who wants to understand more about how it works (for example, its structure, its themes, its techniques)

PURPOSE: to interpret the meaning of a work and the techniques by which that meaning is revealed

Formulate a thesis

The thesis of the literary essay should be something that helps the reader make sense of the work in question.

For example, in Daniel Defoe's *Moll Flanders*, the reader needs to know whether Defoe is purposely ironic or merely accidentally so. Your viewpoint on this question will determine your entire interpretation of the work's meaning.

Find your thesis by asking yourself what the important questions are about the literary work you have in front of you. Sometimes these will be assigned, but sometimes you will have to find your own questions, based on class discussion and reading.

Remember that you cannot conclusively prove your thesis statement. All you are expected to do is to show that your reasons for it are based on the text itself.

Read the work closely

With your working thesis in mind, read the work carefully. Underlining or highlighting the text as you go along is often a good idea (provided you own it, of course).

Note anything that might count as evidence for your analysis of the characteristics of a literary work. Don't, however, neglect passages that might support a contrary view. You will need to account for these as well.

Use secondary sources

Maintain your balance when using secondary sources. Use them to get some critical perspective on the work in question, but remember that your own task is no different than theirs. The main reason for writing a literary essay is to show your own powers of analysis.

Keep track of the sources you have consulted. The ideas you find must be acknowledged to avoid charges of plagiarism. Keep track also of the basic line of argument set forth by each critic you consult: it is unfair to take ideas or phrasing if you intend to use them out of their original context.

Select only the best evidence

After close reading, you need to "back off" from the work somewhat. Your task is not to summarize the work, nor to explain every detail of it, but merely to present a viewpoint that suggests what the work means and how it is put together.

Skim through the work noting down the most prominent support you have found. Then, categorize the material into sections appropriate for discussion in your essay. Fit these into a rough outline, and you are ready to write.

Example

Thesis statement: "Defoe is deliberately ironic in *Moll Flanders*."

A. Moll is a figure of fun, not a serious penitent.
B. Defoe chooses first-person narration for its revelatory advantages.
C. Defoe is deliberately sensational.

To show that Defoe is deliberately ironic in *Moll Flanders*, you might develop the last point by showing the comic sensationalism of the title page as evidence of his ironic purpose.

As you gather support, try not to include everything. Pick only those passages central to an understanding of the work's meaning and those that work best as illustrations of your thesis.

Quote often, but not at great length

The best illustration of a point in a literary essay is a quotation. Whereas paraphrase may be a useful way of reporting research, the quotation is the most precise way to examine meaning in literature. Exactitude is important.

Remember, though, that you must *use* your quotations. Don't just copy them and assume that your point has been made. Focus in on them to show exactly how they work as support for your thesis. Don't assume that the meaning of the quotations or your purpose in quoting them is self-evident.

Write in the present tense

When discussing a work of literature, stay in the present tense—treat the work as a living thing.

Example

Moll rationalizes her theft of the little girl's necklace.

Write with both text and argument in mind

Stay close to the text at all times. But remember that you are not writing to record the plot or to state the obvious. Use the primary text to *demonstrate* your thesis and present your support for the argument at every step of the way.

Write an analysis, not an appreciation or a summary. Don't, for example, waste words admiring Defoe's skill as a novelist. Instead, show how a particular literary work is put together and explain why it has the effect it does.

Assume that the work has unity and coherence, unless evidence shows otherwise. Take the text apart and show how some features of it work. Your job is to show how its synthesis is achieved.

Revise with style

In a literary essay, style is crucial. Your grade will depend not only on what you say but also on how you say it. Check for grace in style. Aim at writing smoothly and confidently. Find a critic you admire and emulate his or her method of proceeding. Your argument, no matter how cogent, will not succeed unless your paper is written well.

■ The Book Review—Essay as Critic

Let such teach others who themselves excel,
And censure freely who have written well.
Alexander Pope

Most of the book reviews you will be asked to write have a more specific purpose than the kind you see in newspapers and magazines. You will be asked not only to report on the content of a book and to evaluate it, but also to analyze it in terms of its contribution to the discipline. A book review gives you a chance to examine one potential source in a given area, often as a prelude to writing a research essay. Like any other essay, it demands a thesis statement that clarifies your reaction to the book.

If you are asked to review a book as part of a course requirement, select a book with a subject matter that appeals to you and with which you feel comfortable. Proceed according to the following stages:

1. Describe or summarize the contents of the book
2. Describe and evaluate its tactics
3. Consider its contribution
4. Illustrate your argument
5. Maintain your critical balance

To write a focused book review, remember your role as fair-minded and helpful critic.

■ The Role of the Book Review

Like other essays, the book review's form is determined by its readers and its function.

AUDIENCE: someone who has not read the book, but who is interested in its subject matter and has some background in the discipline

PURPOSE: to summarize, analyze, and evaluate a book, and to show your critical acumen in so doing; then, to recommend, to criticize, or to dismiss the book according to careful judgment.

(Because these guidelines apply to all books, both fiction and non-fiction, examples have been omitted to avoid confusion.)

Describe the book

1. Determine the thesis of the book (if it is a critical text), the theme (or general meaning) of the book (if it is not), and the audience for which the book is intended.
2. Summarize the book's contents briefly, without giving the show away.
3. Use the book's preface, introduction, and table of contents as a rough guide for your discussion of the work.
4. Discuss the general purpose of the book, without getting caught up in too much detail.

Describe and evaluate the book's tactics

1. If the book is a critical text, describe its method of argument. If it is not a critical text, describe the techniques by which the material is presented.
2. Note how well the book does what it sets out to do.
3. Note what else might have been done or what might have been done differently.
4. Note why you liked (or disliked) the book.

Consider the book's contribution

1. Compare the book to others you have read with a similar thesis or theme.
2. Ask yourself what you learned from the book.

Illustrate your argument

1. At every step of the way, use snippets from the book to back up your position and to give the reader a taste of the work.
2. Include both positive and negative illustrations, unless, of course, your review is entirely positive or negative (rarely the case).
3. Be sure to integrate your illustrations from the book as part of your argument, and not simply as decoration.

Maintain your critical balance

1. Don't be intimidated by ideas just because they are in print. Your object is to assess the merits of the book in question.
2. Don't be too harsh in your judgments. Remember that the author deserves mercy as well as justice.

■ The Research Essay—Essay as Explorer

> We shall not cease from exploration
> And the end of all our exploring
> Will be to arrive where we started
> And know the place for the first time.
>
> *T. S. Eliot*

A research paper is a formal essay based on your exploration of other people's ideas, rather than simply an analysis of your own thoughts. Although both the expository essay and the persuasive essay may use source material to some extent, the research essay is unique. Its purpose is to formulate a thesis based on a survey and assessment of source material.

The following steps are essential to the development of a research paper:

1. Mapping out the area of exploration
2. Finding a working bibliography
3. Drawing up an outline
4. Recording source material
5. Writing and documenting your essay

■ The Role of the Research Paper

A research paper must be modified to suit its readers and its special aims.

AUDIENCE: an informed, curious reader, whom you address on a professional level

PURPOSE: to show your skill in exploring, evaluating, and recording source material in a manner that shows how you have synthesized it

Mapping out the area of exploration

Before you begin to explore the library, you must find an area that is appropriate for investigation. A good research topic will have the following characteristics:

1. **Scope.** Your subject should be neither too broad nor too narrow in its focus.

   Example: "The Sonnet"—too broad
   "The Petrarchan Sonnet"—not focused enough
   "The Petrarchan Sonnet as a subject of Renaissance satire"
   —more focused

2. **Support.** Your subject must be treated in written sources that are available to you. For example, a recent subject may not be a good choice because there may not yet be enough written about it. Also, remember that your sources must be treated objectively, so that the final paper reflects what is

known about a subject, rather than just what you believe to be true about a subject. For example, the thesis "The Petrarchan Sonnet is unreadable today" is based upon uninformed opinion and is *not* a good subject for a research paper.

3. **Significance.** Find something that you want to explore and that needs exploration. For example, the topic "The History of the Petrarchan Sonnet" is not enough in question to be a significant subject for a research essay. But "The Influence of Petrarch on English Poetry—its Benefits and Shortcomings" is a subject that allows a good deal of scope for significant research.

Finding a working bibliography

Read widely at first to locate the best sources. Then read deeply in order to get at the heart of the matter. Explore the topic with your tentative thesis in mind, revising it as you go along.

1. Find general information in an encyclopedia, dictionary, or other reference book. The list in the Appendix offers some places to start.
2. Find information in the library computer system, microfiche, or card catalogue. Look under the subject heading or use the names of authors or titles that you have found in any of the encyclopedias you consulted.

   For example, to find information on Petrarch and the sonnet tradition that he fathered, look up PETRARCH and SONNET under the subject heading in the library card catalogue.
3. Consult periodical indexes for further information. Often the periodical will give you more current material than is available in books. Some indexes are listed in the Appendix.
4. As an alternative to looking through indexes and abstracts for information on a subject, you can have a search performed for you by computer. Most college and university libraries have an on-line search service.

   The advantages of a computer search are that it is quick, thorough, and up-to-date. In most college and university libraries, there is a charge for having this service performed. Although there are many factors which affect the cost of a search, such as the complexity of the search strategy, the cost of the database(s) searched, the number of references found and printed, and even the time of day, most searches required by an undergraduate student should cost between $5 and $15. Your library's on-line searcher can usually give you an estimate before beginning the search.

   The whole field of using computers to find information is changing very rapidly. The best way to know what is happening RIGHT NOW is to ask your reference librarian, who will bring you up-to-date on the technology and, more importantly, the choices available in your particular college or university library.
5. Examine your sources with your specific topic in mind. Check the table of contents and the index of the books you find to search for suitable material.
6. Note down bibliographical information for any of the sources you consult.

Small note cards (3" x 5") are useful. Record the library call numbers for your sources.

7. Follow the rules of documentation that apply to your discipline at this stage, and you will save time and trouble toward the end. Some guides to acceptable documentation are listed in the Appendix.

Although the sample research essay shown in this book is in the style of the Modern Language Association, some disciplines demand other styles of documentation. Consult your instructor if in doubt.

SAMPLE BIBLIOGRAPHY CARD

Gibaldi, Joseph, and Walter S. Achtert. MLA Handbook for Writers of Research Papers. 2nd. ed. New York: Modern Language Association, 1984.

Drawing up an outline

An outline for a research essay takes its direction from your preparatory reading. Follow the instructions given earlier on how to design an outline with these precautions in mind:

1. Your outline must be flexible enough to accommodate all the information pertinent to your thesis statement.
2. Your outline must be fair and must reflect an objective approach to the material.
3. Your outline must be firmly established in your mind so that it does not attempt to include more material than can be adequately handled within the limits of the assignment.
4. Your outline is designed to be used. In the case of a research essay, the outline dictates the direction of your note-taking. It should help you stay on track in your explorations and help you limit yourself to what is possible.

Recording source material

Like an explorer, you must accurately record the steps of your journey. You need a system. Here are some suggestions to simplify the task:

1. Take notes on large index cards (4" x 6" should do).

2. Identify the source on each card as briefly as possible. Usually, a last name and a page number will do.
3. Quote or paraphrase as the occasion demands (remember that too much quotation is dull). In addition, paraphrasing as you read will help you make sense of the material.
4. Limit yourself generally to one note per card to make sorting easier. This tactic will keep you from unconsciously relying too heavily on any one source.
5. Sort through your material at intervals to decide where it will fit into your working outline. If it won't fit, revise the outline or throw the irrelevant information out—no matter how attractive it is.
6. Copy accurately. If the passage is very lengthy, photocopy it to ensure precision.

Why bother?

Note-taking is such a painful chore that it is tempting not to do it. Don't succumb to the temptation. Note-taking is an essential part of research. It will help you determine the value of your sources. Ask these questions as you take notes:

1. Are the sources reliable?
2. Are they recent?
3. Are the sources themselves respected and well reviewed by others?
4. What are your own reactions to the sources?

This last point shows the need to record your own reactions to source material as you proceed. Add these ideas to your note cards to help you develop ideas later. You can differentiate them from source material by adding your initials.

Remember, the object of research is not to record facts, but to evaluate and synthesize your findings about an unsettled matter according to the viewpoint or thesis of your paper.

Writing and documenting your essay

Prepare an outline, complete with intended patterns of argument, as suggested earlier in this text. Then, write the first draft of your essay's introduction, body, and conclusion. This time, however, you must make sure to acknowledge your debt to any source as you write. One good way to do so is to include an abbreviated version of the source in parentheses immediately following the quoted matter in your essay.

Example

The only avenue left to the poets of this period was "to seek models in modern literatures. Of these, the Italian most naturally suggested itself, since the Cinquecento was the flourishing time of the Italian Renaissance in politics, art, and literature" (Berdan 702).

This example not only shows the ease of abbreviation, but demonstrates the ease of the MLA style of documentation. It is also an example of the benefits of good preliminary note-taking.

For more information on documentation in MLA and APA style, see Chapter 16.

Control

The special challenge of the research paper is to handle your source material in a controlled way. To control your research essay, remember these guidelines:

1. **Keep it limited.** Qualify the aim of your essay and stay within the limits of the thesis and the assignment.

2. **Keep it concise.** Avoid pretentious diction.
   (See Chapter 12 for more information.)

3. **Keep it formal.** This suggestion may even mean that you should not use the pronoun "I," in order to maintain objectivity (although it is often acceptable to do so). Ask your instructor for specific advice on this point.

4. **Keep it clean.** Small errors reduce the essay's credibility as an accurate record of research.

5. **Make it yours.** Don't lose yourself in assembled bits of research. Assimilate the material. Learn from it. What you include and how you use it determine your success as a researcher.

■ Sample Research Essay

The following is a sample research essay whose format conforms to the new MLA guidelines. Study it carefully, noting the format and the method of documentation.

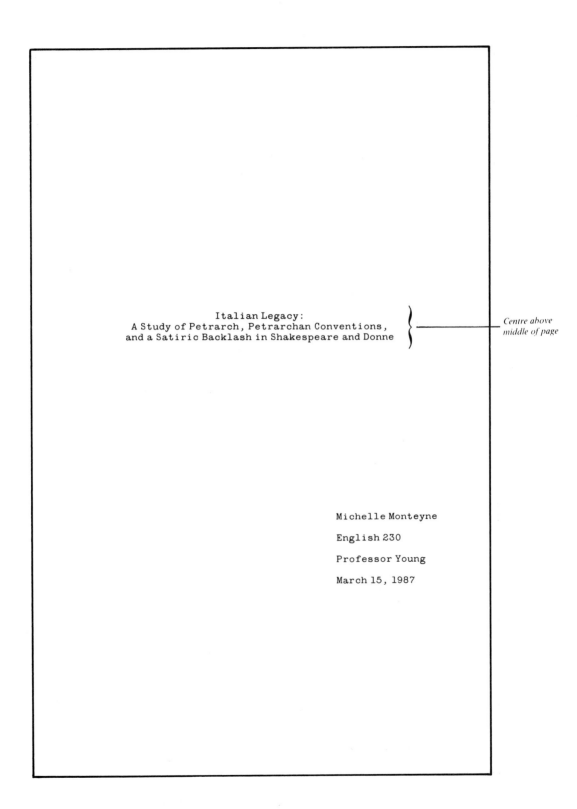

Italian Legacy:
A Study of Petrarch, Petrarchan Conventions,
and a Satiric Backlash in Shakespeare and Donne

*Centre above
middle of page*

Michelle Monteyne

English 230

Professor Young

March 15, 1987

Outline

Thesis: Petrarch's love sonnets influenced English poetry
mainly in the satiric treatment that the conventions
received from Renaissance poets such as Donne and
Shakespeare.

Introduction: Petrarch's contribution to English poetry is
misunderstood. He did not invent the sonnet, nor did his
poetry in translation have a direct effect on English
poetry.

I. Source of the Petrarchan influence in England
    A. Brought to England by Sir Thomas Wyatt
    B. Influenced writers because of the transitional state
        of English poetry
    C. Influenced English writers because of the
        flourishing of the Italian Renaissance

II. Three strains of Petrarchan influence
    A. Petrarchism--sincere imitation or translation
    B. Petrarchismo--slavish imitation using rigid
        conventions
    C. Anti-petrarchan movement

III. Poets playing with the conventions of idealized beauty
     and love
    A. Shakespeare--Sonnet 130
    B. Donne--''The Apparition''
    C. Donne--''Love's Alchemy''
    D. Shakespeare--Sonnet 73

Conclusion: Petrarch and Petrarchan conventions had a great
influence on English poetry, even though the idealism of
the earlier poetry served as a target for satire.

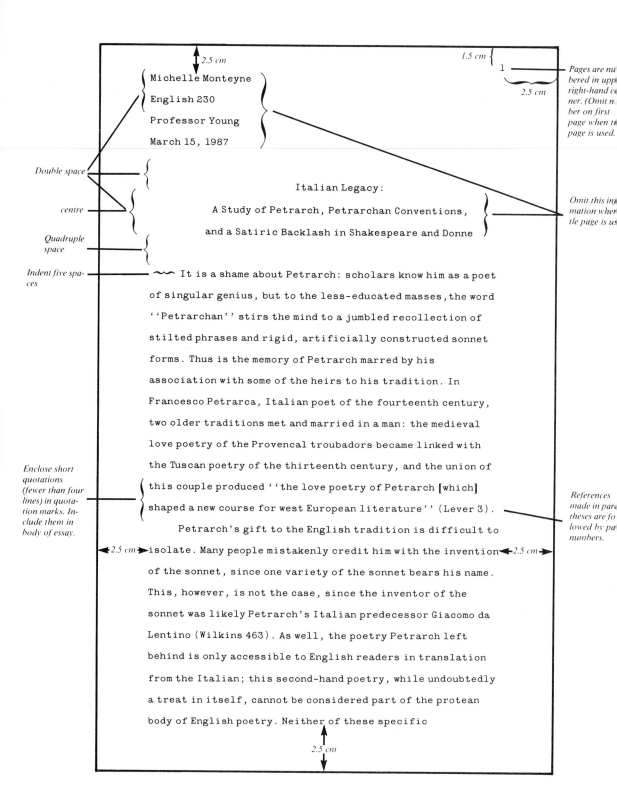

2.5 cm

1.5 cm

1

2.5 cm

Michelle Monteyne

English 230

Professor Young

March 15, 1987

Pages are numbered in upper right-hand corner. (Omit number on first page when title page is used.

Double space

centre

Italian Legacy:

A Study of Petrarch, Petrarchan Conventions,

and a Satiric Backlash in Shakespeare and Donne

Omit this information when title page is used

Quadruple space

Indent five spaces

It is a shame about Petrarch: scholars know him as a poet of singular genius, but to the less-educated masses, the word ''Petrarchan'' stirs the mind to a jumbled recollection of stilted phrases and rigid, artificially constructed sonnet forms. Thus is the memory of Petrarch marred by his association with some of the heirs to his tradition. In Francesco Petrarca, Italian poet of the fourteenth century, two older traditions met and married in a man: the medieval love poetry of the Provencal troubadors became linked with the Tuscan poetry of the thirteenth century, and the union of this couple produced ''the love poetry of Petrarch [which] shaped a new course for west European literature'' (Lever 3).

Enclose short quotations (fewer than four lines) in quotation marks. Include them in body of essay.

References made in parentheses are followed by page numbers.

Petrarch's gift to the English tradition is difficult to

◄2.5 cm► isolate. Many people mistakenly credit him with the invention ◄2.5 cm► of the sonnet, since one variety of the sonnet bears his name. This, however, is not the case, since the inventor of the sonnet was likely Petrarch's Italian predecessor Giacomo da Lentino (Wilkins 463). As well, the poetry Petrarch left behind is only accessible to English readers in translation from the Italian; this second-hand poetry, while undoubtedly a treat in itself, cannot be considered part of the protean body of English poetry. Neither of these specific

2.5 cm

contributions has given Petrarch his place in the journals of English literary history. His legacy is rather one of more broad, sweeping proportions: he gave to English literature a tradition of courtly love-sonnets that acted as a springboard for many great poets of the sixteenth and seventeenth centuries.

There is some disagreement about the placement, so to speak, of Petrarch's prolific seed in England's vessel. The consensus, however, seems to be that Sir Thomas Wyatt, in his Italian wanderings, brought the form home, both in translation and in the creation of original verse, and that this form was later adopted and improved upon by Henry Howard, Earl of Surrey. W. L. Bullock, for instance, believes that

> the most natural hypothesis for the origin of the English sonnet form is the theory that Surrey gave its final permanent shape by relaxing and simplifying the type which Wyatt had adopted as the one among the various Italian models least foreign to the nature and the existing forms of English poetry. (Bullock 743)

Indent long quotations (four or more lines) ten spaces; omit quotation marks.

It is J. M. Berdan, however, who theorizes as to why, at this time, England was ready for this kind of foreign influence in its literature. ''At the opening of the sixteenth century,'' he says, ''the English language was in a state of transition.'' Various changes were occurring in spelling, grammar, and pronunciation. As a result, poets of this period who were ''attempting to follow Chaucer in a non-Chaucerian age and in a non-Chaucerian language . . . were foredoomed to failure.'' The return to the Latin and Greek classics did not

Integrate quotations into sentences where possible.

have a great effect on the poetry of this early period, Berdan goes on to say, since ''the humanist impulse was not the main factor in Tudor poetry.'' The only avenue left to the poets of this period, therefore, was ''to seek models in modern literature. Of these, the Italian most naturally suggested itself, since the Cinquecento was the flourishing time of the Italian Renaissance in politics, art, and literature'' (Berdan 699-702).

The reverberations of Petrarch's influence can be traced in two main streams of English literary history:

> First, Petrarchism, where the author, carried away by his admiration, unconsciously and not servilely copies his master, or honestly translates him. Secondly, Petrarchismo . . . an insincere literary fashion, where Petrarch figures only as the first of the type. Examples of this are any of the Elizabethan sonneteers. (Berdan 704)

It is this second strain, the so-called Petrarchismo, that is most well known today, and Berdan had very good reason for branding it insincere, for it is poetry somehow removed from the heart, displaced from the soul of the poet. Marius Pieri gives a more explicit description:

> Petrarchismo is the art of treating cleverly and wittily matters of the heart, of composing love-poems without the emotion in the soul, of feigning passion for an imaginary mistress, and of singing a fiction of amorous intrigue, whose phases and whose stages are fixed, and, as it were, established by an immovable tradition. (Berdan 704)

The labelling of Elizabethan poetry as an ''insincere'' copy of Petrarch's model does not mean that it is not good poetry; bad poetry abounds in sonnet form as it does in other genres, but some of the finest poetry in the English language was created by poets writing within this tradition. However, it is also true that a great deal of brilliant poetry was written <u>against</u> this tradition. Many poets have played with the style, structure, language, and conventions that came from Petrarch and were embellished by later writers. Two of the most famous English poets, William Shakespeare and John Donne, found no end of delight in mocking the ''Petrarchan'' conventions of their day.

I have chosen to speak about Shakespeare and Donne because they are the most skillful poets to play against this tradition. But they were not alone. ''There was, in fact, in these years [the 1590's], a tremendous outbreak of satirical writing, and one of the favourite targets of this satire was the amorous sonneteer. Both the fashion and its antidote arose almost simultaneously'' (Cruttwell 19). J. B. Leishman speaks of this phenomenon, remarking that

> a new generation . . . [was] reacting against most of
> the literary ideals and fashions which had
> hitherto prevailed, and declaring, in so many
> words, that it is time to get down from one's
> stilts, to remove one's rose-coloured spectacles,
> and to see things as they really are. (Leishman 41)

Among the poets to join in the fun were John Marston and Joseph Hall (Cruttwell 19).

One of the easiest targets for attack in this kind of

Use an ellipsis to indicate words omitted.

Use square brackets to add words needed for clarity.

poetry has always been the convention of the idyllic beauty of the mistress to whom the sonnet is generally addressed. The importance of the image of ''woman'' cannot be overemphasized when discussing Petrarchan conventions. ''Belief in a fundamental rapport between nature and the human spirit, and in woman as the mystic channel, through which this passed, is at the core of the romance tradition'' (Lever 7). Of all the satiric poetry to come out of this period, Shakespeare's Sonnet 130 must be the most killing on the issue of female beauty:

> My mistress' eyes are nothing like the sun;
> Coral is far more red than her lips red;
> If snow be white, why then her breasts are dun;
> If hairs be wires, black wires grow on her head.
> I have seen roses damasked, red and white,
> But no such roses see I in her cheeks;
> And in some perfumes is there more delight
> Than in the breath that from my mistress reeks.
> I love to hear her speak; yet well I know
> That music hath a far more pleasing sound:
> I grant I never saw a goddess go;
> My mistress, when she walks, treds on the ground.
>   And yet, by heaven, I think my love as rare
>   As any she belied with false compare.
> (Shakespeare 1475)

In this poem we see every possible descriptive convention satirized: eyes, lips, hair, even breath! Patrick Cruttwell discusses this poem in connection with the model that it comes from, the seventh poem in Thomas Watson's

<u>Passionate Centurie of Love</u>. He shows each line of Watson next to Shakespeare's mocking echo. This juxtaposition speaks for itself; there is no doubt that Shakespeare wanted to tear apart the convention of ideal female beauty. But why did he want to do so: simply for the sake of proving the convention to be rigid, outdated, and silly? I do not think so. Certainly he wanted to expose the folly of this kind of hyperbole, but more importantly, he used this convention to help him write a better love poem. After ridiculing Petrarchan conventions in the first twelve lines, he takes a radically different tone in the rhyming couplet: the ironic voice disappears completely, to be replaced by a voice of tender, soft, serious love. Shakespeare mocks romantic conventions and insults the ''mistress'' in an almost alarming way, yet, in spite of this treatment, the loving tribute of the last two lines is as moving as a courtly love sonnet ever could be. He brings the woman down to earth, has her ''tread on the ground,'' as it were. But this casting away of the ''rose-coloured spectacles'' has the effect of raising this lady much higher, in the end, than if she had been deified all along.

John Donne uses the Petrarchan conventions in much the same way that Shakespeare does; in fact, these conventions often form the bases for his characteristic ''metaphysical conceits.'' In his poem, ''The Apparition,'' for example, Donne plays on the familiar idea that the mistress can kill her lover with looks of scorn. With his unique and restless imagination, Donne conjures up a vision of his mistress tortured by fear after she has ''killed'' him:

Underline book titles in essay and in list of works cited.

Enclose titles of short works (not published under separate cover) in quotation marks.

When by thy scorn, O murd'ress, I am dead,

   And that thou thinkst thee free

From all solicitation from me,

Then shall my ghost come to thy bed,

And thee, fained vestal, in worse arms shall see;

Then thy sick taper will begin to wink,

And he, whose thou art then, being tired before,

Will, if thou stir, or pinch to wake him, think

    Thou call'st for more,

And in false sleep will from thee shrink,

And then, poor aspen wretch, neglected thou

Bathed in a cold quicksilver sweat wilt lie,

   A verier ghost than I;

What I will say, I will not tell thee now,

Lest that preserve thee; and since my love is

    spent,

I had rather thou shouldst painfully repent,

Than by my threat'nings rest still innocent.

   (Donne 27)

Among the horrors that she faces after his death are a lesser lover (''worse arms'') and the ghost of Donne himself. This, of course, is an utterly brilliant twist to give to the exaggerated convention, and only Donne could twist it in such a way. It is more than just wit. Donne uses the convention advantageously to berate the mistress for her scorn, neglect, and infidelity. The rhyming couplet at the close changes tone just as the couplet ending Shakespeare's 130th Sonnet does.

   Another of Donne's poems that contains an element of anti-Petrarchan ridicule is ''Love's Alchemy.'' In this poem, we find the following lines:

> That loving wretch that swears
> 'Tis not the bodies marry, but the minds,
> Which he in her angelic finds,
> Would swear as justly, that he hears,
> In that day's rude hoarse minstrelsy, the spheres.
>
> (Donne 22)

This excerpt, when taken in the context of the poem, confirms a generally cynical, misogynistic feeling. Donne is angry with women again, or at least angry with one woman in particular, and a succinct summing up of the poem could probably be found in the phrase, ''Hope not for mind in women.'' This is Donne's point, but he chooses to deliver it in such a way that it disparages not only women, but, as well, the idea of a purely spiritual, non-physical love. This notion is one of the primary tenets of courtly love poetry, and it finds its origin, as do the other conventions, in the poetry of Petrarch. Of the Italian poet, J. W. Lever says,

> Life shaped the course of his literary work, and
> the years he spent in Avignon fixed a permanent
> mark on his genius. Here, in the city where the new
> Italian humanism met the fading culture of
> medieval Provence, Petrarch first set eyes on the
> burgher's daughter Madonna Laura. For the rest of
> his life the roots of his imagination were to
> fasten themselves round an imperishable, forever
> unattainable love. . . . Laura was indeed the living
> manifestation of heavenly virtue. (Lever 3)

This kind of idealized vision might have worked in the poems of Petrarch, but Donne thought that it had been carried too far. Just as the true ''elixir'' of love can never be found (that is, there is no ideal love), so there is no ideal woman. In his poetry, the choice of imagery bears out this belief. Donne chooses real images from the experiences of everyday life: the sciences, travel, and current philosophies (Grierson 26). This kind of imagery is another departure from the courtly language of conventional love poems.

The images in Shakespeare's poems are also quite different from those of their courtly ancestors. The notion of time's passage is a strong theme that runs through many a Shakespearean sonnet. Herbert Grierson discusses this issue: he believes that something

> had come over this idealist and courtly love-
> poetry by the end of the sixteenth century.
> . . . This poetry had begun to absorb a new warmth
> and spirit, not from Petrarch and medieval
> chivalry, but from classical love-poetry. . . . The
> courtly, idealistic strain was crossed by an
> Epicurean and sensuous one that . . . echoes again
> and again the Pagan cry, never heard in Dante or
> Petrarch, of the fleetingness of beauty and of
> love. . . . (Grierson 26)

The best example of this theme in Shakespeare's collection of sonnets is the 73rd:

> That time of year thou mayst in me behold
> When yellow leaves, or none, or few, do hang
> Upon those boughs which shake against the cold,

> Bare ruined choirs where late the sweet birds
>
> > sang.
>
> In me thou see'st the twilight of such day
>
> As after sunset fadeth in the west,
>
> Which by and by black night doth take away,
>
> Death's second self that seals up all in rest.
>
> In me thou see'st the glowing of such fire
>
> That on the ashes of his youth doth lie,
>
> As the deathbed whereon it must expire,
>
> Consumed with that which it was nourished by.
>
> > This thou perceiv'st, which makes thy love more
> >
> > > strong,
> >
> > To love that well which thou must leave ere
> >
> > > long. (Shakespeare 1465)

There are three main images in this poem: images of autumn, of sunset, and of fire. All of these images concern the end of a cycle--death really--except the curious paradox of the fire. These images would all be out of place in a conventional love poem. Yet the use of death-like, time-consumed images is explained in the last one--fire. The fire consumes itself by the very strength of its passionate burning. In the same way, we know that our lives on earth must be short because we love so strongly while we are here. This passionate love that Shakespeare captures is a far cry from the idealized love-at-a-distance that is found in much of the courtly poetry. This love is just as strong as the conventional kind, but it looks all the better in the absence of the ''rose-coloured spectacles.''

This strongly anti-Petrarchan tradition might appear to

some to be unduly hard on Petrarch. But at this point it would be wise to remember that it is the conventions that Shakespeare, Donne, and some others were mocking, not Petrarch, nor his poems. Though by the end of the sixteenth century, the Petrarchan worship had decreased somewhat from the time when Ascham commented that ''men have in more reverence the <u>Triumphs</u> of Petrarch, than the Genesis of Moses'' (834), Petrarch was still read and widely admired. It is ever thus in a world where imitation is considered ''the sincerest form of flattery,'' but the imitators are weak, unwise, and unskilled. And in our far-removed modern world of often graphic realism, it is much easier to believe in the real than the ideal, and to laugh in agreement over Shakespeare's startling lines: ''Men have died from time to time, and worms have eaten them, but not for love'' (<u>As You Like It</u> 4.1.101-02).

Use Arabic numerals to show act, scene, and line divisions.

Works Cited

Ascham, Roger. The Schoolmaster in The Renaissance in
England. Eds. H. E. Rollins and H. Baker. Lexington: D.
C. Heath, 1954.

Berdan, J. M. ''A Definition of Petrarchismo.'' PMLA 24
(1909): 699-710.

Bullock, W. L. ''Genesis of the English Sonnet Form.'' PMLA 38
(1923): 729-44.

Cruttwell, Patrick. The Shakespearean Moment and Its Place in
the Poetry of the 17th Century. London: Chatto and
Windus, 1954.

Donne, John. John Donne's Poetry. Ed. A. L. Clements. New
York: Norton, 1966.

Grierson, Herbert. ''Donne's Love-Poetry.'' John Donne: A
Collection of Critical Essays. Ed. Helen Gardner. New
Jersey: Prentice-Hall, 1962.

Leishman, J. B. Introduction. The Three Parnasus Plays.
Herts: Ivor, Nicholson & Watson, 1949.

Lever, J. W. The Elizabethan Love Sonnet. London: Methuen,
1966.

Shakespeare, William. William Shakespeare: The Complete
Works. Ed. Alfred Harbage. 1969. Baltimore: Penguin,
1972.

---. As You Like It. Ed. Albert Gilman. Scarborough: New
American Library, 1963.

Wilkins, E. H. ''The Invention of the Sonnet.'' MPhil 13
(1915): 463-69.

List only works
cited in essay.

List according
to last name in
alphabetical or-
der.

Periodical re-
ferences must
include com-
plete page num-
bers when listed
in Works Cited.

Abbreviate pub-
lication infor-
mation without
sacrificing clar-
ity.

Make sure list
of works cited
matches each
reference in
body of essay.

Use three hy-
phens plus a pe-
riod to avoid re-
peating author's
name.

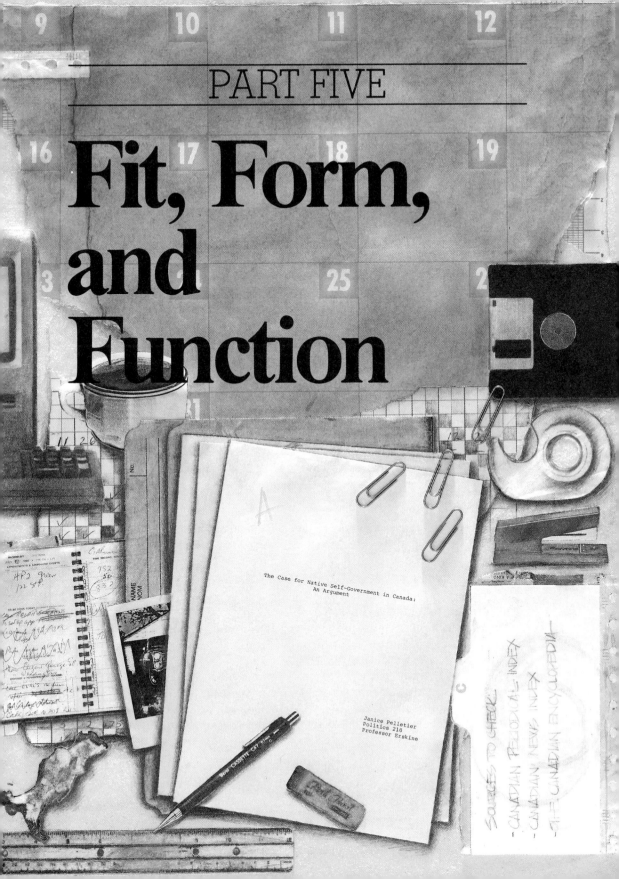

PART FIVE

Fit, Form, and Function

The Case for Native Self-Government in Canada:
An Argument

Janice Pelletier
Politics 210
Professor Erskine

Choosing Words

Such labored nothings, in so strange a style
Amaze th' unlearned, and make the learned smile.
Alexander Pope

Word choice is perhaps the most accurate index of the status of a writer. The words you choose depend in part on the role you mean to play in relation to the reader.

Example

A memo from a superior might read:

Employees are to limit lunch breaks to no more than thirty minutes.

The effect of such impersonal language is to distance the boss from the employee; although the boss may sign the memo, there is no suggestion in the language itself that the words are related to him or her.

Alternate Example

Say that you receive a letter addressed directly to you with the following message:

Dear Employee: I don't want you to take more than thirty minutes for lunch ever again. Signed, The Boss.

Although the import of the message is the same, the impact is quite different. In this case, the order does not seem to come from "on high." This time, you might perhaps take the note very personally and storm into the boss's office, feeling entitled to an explanation.

The more distanced note, on the other hand, sounds so impersonal that you might be less inclined to resent it directly and much more intimidated by the distance imposed by your superior.

The first note is not necessarily better than the other, but it would probably achieve the desired result: supreme control over the employees.

What determines the success of a style is not its beauty or power in isolation, but its impact, the response that it gets, and the relationship it forms with the reader.

Write to impress—not to intimidate

When you write an essay, the style you seek is different from that of a boss to an employee. You should address your reader as an equal; the information you impart and the viewpoint you defend are offered as reasonable choices for readers as clear thinking as you are.

To impress a reader, you need to show what you know and to express a willingness to share it. If your words do not allow you to share your results, either because they are too technical, or too vague or carelessly chosen, you will have alienated your readers. Remember that in the formal essay, the emphasis is less upon you and the reader personally than it is upon the subject at hand: your relationship is entirely professional. But in the informal essay, your personality and that of your reader play more pronounced roles: you expect that the reader will enjoy your company.

Make yourself comfortable in the language of your subject

Determining your status, and thus the proper diction for an essay, is sometimes a great challenge. After all, you may not feel much like the equal of the professor giving a course in which you feel shaky or ill prepared. Obviously, the more conversant you become with the terminology of a discipline, the easier it will be to feel like an equal and to write a stimulating learned discussion.

Just as important, however, is the confidence with which you can play the role of an equal. Think of your paper not as just another assignment, written by a student to a professor, but as an opportunity to speak the language of the discipline to someone who understands it.

Choose your words stylishly

The "rules" which govern diction cannot be listed here, simply because word choice depends upon context. A formal essay demands formal language, just as a formal occasion demands evening dress. Likewise, informal writing allows you more freedom in self-expression and a more casual approach.

■ Diction: Fit, Form, and Function

Choose language that satisfies the criteria of fit, form, and function for the assignment in question. What follows are some pointers on how to choose (and to revise) the language of your essays.

Observing the dress code

Paying attention to the conventions of a dress code does not mean that you must wear a uniform inhibiting all expression of personality. It means, simply, that you must conform to certain standards, happily, in this case, quite flexible standards.

Keep these guidelines in mind:

1. Fit—Does your writing suit its purpose and audience?
2. Form—Does it conform to convention?
3. Function—Does your writing make your message clear?

If the idea of conforming for the sake of conforming disturbs you, remember what the consequences of not conforming may be: perhaps being misunderstood, ignored, or considered offensive.

To avoid any of these perils in your use of language and in your word choice particularly, keep these hints in mind.

Avoid over-dressed language

1. Do not use too many technical or specialized terms.

Too many terms may actually prevent your reader from seeing your underlying meaning. Technical subjects clearly demand some technical terminology, but while it is partly your task to demonstrate your ability to use terms with skill and ease, you must not use them to confuse your reader or to avoid the issues.

Example

Avoid use of these words out of their normal context.

X "feedback"   X "output"   X "interface"

Beware of words that end in "ize" and "ization."

X "finalize"   Replace with "finish" or "complete."

2. Avoid pretentious words and constructions.

Often these pretentious constructions appear as groups of nouns, attached in such a way that the reader cannot visualize the object described. The tendency to use such abstract and depersonalized language comes partly from our desire to appear sophisticated, but the effect is rather like wearing designer labels on the outside of our clothes. Such a high-sounding style may intimidate or amuse, but it does not really communicate.

Example

X *His close scrutinization of the exam terrified him: he hated essay questions.*

Replace "scrutinization" with "scrutiny." Guard against many of the "words" that end in "ize" or "ization."

3. Avoid "flashy" words.

Sometimes a student will fervently consult a thesaurus seeking some clever ways of varying vocabulary. Although this is a commendable practice, never forget that no two words mean exactly the same thing or have precisely the same impact. When you find a synonym, check it out in the dictionary to make sure that it means what you think it does. Make sure your words know their place.

A longer word is not necessarily a stronger word. A word selected simply "for show" may be as out of place as a diamond tiara worn with a soccer uniform. Context is the first consideration in these matters. Don't use a word just because it sounds elevated.

Example

> X At any time of year, upon entering this voluminous structure, one cannot help but notice the low roar of conversation as the voices of the library's patrons reverberate from one concrete wall to the other.

How can a library be "voluminous"? Replace this word with something more suitable—like "huge" or "imposing."

Avoid sloppy language

1. Avoid slang.

There are, admittedly, times when slang fits the mood. You may, for instance, wish to draw attention to the common language for a particular term, or report some dialogue. Beware of enclosing slang in quotation marks ("swell"); it may seem forced and unnatural. Unless you are sure that slang will add colour and character to your writing, avoid it. Careless slang is sloppy and perhaps more revealing than you wish.

Example

> X Modern socialites must wear all the latest fashions to feel that all is truly well with their world, even though this penchant for the latest threads often causes a severe drain on their bank accounts.

Replace "latest threads" with something that matches the tone more effectively.

2. Avoid colloquial constructions.

Colloquial constructions may include slang, but they also include language that is chatty, takes too much for granted, or is not completely clear. A carefully selected colloquial word or phrase may add unexpected life to a formal paper, but the overuse of language generally confined to speech may lead the reader to dismiss the value and importance of what you are saying.

Because you have no chance to reinforce your words with body language (a raised eyebrow, a smile, a frown), your reader will need the most precise, specific language you can possibly find. You need all the power and clarity of words at your command.

Example

> X Nuclear disarmament seems like a pretty good idea.

Replace "pretty good" with something stronger.

3. Avoid saying the obvious, especially in a hackneyed way.

What you have to say may not be entirely new, but your approach to the subject should be fresh and your way of expressing yourself should give the reader a new angle of perception.

Avoid language deadened by overuse, whether it be jargon or cliché. Use language that enlightens, that sparks thought, that provokes discussion, that wakes up your reader. Saying the same old thing in the same old way may be the easy way out, but it will not have the same impact that a thoughtful or inventive use of words may have.

The cliché does, however, have its place. For instance, in the paragraph above, the phrase "the easy way out," is a cliché. In the midst of some fairly abstract prose, its presence can startle just because it is a different kind of language than what precedes it. Use clichés sparingly, and don't use them thoughtlessly. Otherwise they may have all the impact of a joke too often repeated.

Example

> X *Breed registries and associations are in the business of singing their animals' praises, so read their publications critically, if you are planning to buy a horse.*

Replace "singing their animals' praises" with fresher, more thoughtful phrasing.

EXERCISES

1. Make a list of common expressions we use to describe someone who is somewhat lacking in intelligence. (The list should include phrases like "out to lunch.") Analyze these expressions to determine their appeal. Do the same thing with words and expressions we use to describe drunkenness.

2. Find more formal ways of making the following statements, developing the idea more fully in each case:
    a. You're pulling my leg.
    b. She's crying her eyes out.
    c. He'll snap your head off.
    d. Twist my arm.
    e. I'll shake the daylights out of him.
    f. He worked his butt off.
    g. She took the exercises to heart.

3. Our clichés often take the form of comparisons. It was "as cold as ice," "as cool as a cucumber." Make a list of these trite expressions and then vary them by drawing new comparisons.

4. Look up a common adjective in a thesaurus and note five of the variations listed as synonyms. Then check each of them in the dictionary to note the distinctions between them. Use each of them in a sentence that makes the word's special meaning clear.

5. Read over essays you have written and note any clichés or jargon you have used. Try to rephrase them in fresh language.

Reducing Wordiness

> Words are like leaves; and where they most abound,
> Much fruit of sense beneath is rarely found.
>
> *Alexander Pope*

A wordy essay does not necessarily transgress the word limit of the assignment. Rather, it contains extraneous words, contributing nothing to the meaning and draining force from the essay's argument.

Wordy writing is often characteristic of a first draft. It is close to idle chat: though spontaneous and sometimes even fascinating, it lacks direction. It wanders, perhaps arriving eventually at meaning; it does not set out in orderly pursuit of it. A wordy essay is often a sign of poorly revised and overdressed thought.

Make every word fit. If you can make your writing more succinct, your work will be clearer and your reader will be more attentive. A few suggestions for improving the conciseness of your writing are listed below.

■ A Perfect Fit

Avoid visible seams

When talking, we commonly join ideas together randomly. Speed is the goal, not beautiful construction. Consider the following example:

Example

He passed the museum.

You decide to add a further detail.

X *He passed the museum which was on his way home.*

Your new thought shows an obvious seam. "Which" and "that" can often be removed to produce a more graceful line.

✔ *He passed the museum on his way home.*

Avoid frills

Often, a speaker describes something by using words accompanied by adverbs meant to accentuate their effect. Here are some examples:

X quite sure
X extremely unhappy
X very excited

Replace these with:

✔ *certain, convinced*
✔ *desolate*
✔ *exhilarated*

In writing, the search for impact is better served by a stronger word, rather than a modified word. And, in writing, there is time to conduct a search for it. Use that time to dress your thoughts appropriately.

The same advice holds true for redundant wording. Avoid phrases like:

X naive and innocent

Use:

✔ *ingenuous*
✔ *naive*
✔ *innocent*

Naive and innocent mean the same thing. It is unnecessary to use both.

Avoid baggy constructions

A baggy sentence often contains vague words intended to conceal vague thoughts. Such sentences invariably include the following all-too-common words and phrases:

X due to the fact
X an aspect of
X the use of
X being

These can usually be excised completely or at most replaced by a single word. "Because" is an excellent substitute for "due to the fact that."

Tentative language is another frequent cause of bagginess. Avoid using phrases like:

X appears to suggest
X serves to demonstrate
X acts as a remedy

Substitute:

✔ *suggests*
✔ *demonstrates*
✔ *remedies*

Avoid the "grand style"

Writing in the "grand style" uses pompous phrasing to clothe modest ideas. Pompous introductions are a common source of the problem:

X It is this theory which needs . . .
✔ This theory needs . . .
X It was his view that . . .
✔ He thought that . . .

Avoid excessive formality

Just as you wouldn't wear evening dress to compete in a bowling tournament, so you should not use static language to describe active thoughts.

Where possible, keep sentences in their typical order—use the active voice, and move from subject to verb to object. "The Prime Minister gave the order" is a much more direct statement than the passive construction, "The order was given by the Prime Minister."

X A decision was made by the committee to conduct further studies.
✔ The committee decided to conduct further studies.

While the passive mode has its uses (as discussed earlier), it *is* wordier, less forceful, and generally harder to understand. It is all talk and no action. When revising, keep a watchful eye on the number of times you resort to the static passive voice. It can occasionally serve as a tactful way of avoiding direct confrontation.

Example
_____

PASSIVE: *This amount is owing.* (what the bill says)

ACTIVE: *You owe us this amount.* (what the bill means)

■ Wordiness Analyzed

The preceding examples illustrate that wordiness is most often caused by speech habits not entirely abandoned in writing. To analyze the causes of your own wordiness, note especially any words you use either to *warm up* as you begin to write, to *cover up* your insecurities and uncertainties as you proceed, or to *spruce up* a thought better left unadorned.

■ Preventive Measures

When editing, check to see that your sentences are designed for simplicity, concreteness, action, grace, and impact.

EXERCISE

Improve the following sentences by eliminating redundant words or phrases.

1. The hat that she wore on her head to the Easter service was uniquely one of a kind.
2. The employment counsellor asked Pierre to elaborate on future prospects.
3. The politician claimed that the press was guilty of a factual misrepresentation.

4. The survey ascertained the number of houses in the community that had undergone a burglary experience.
5. Despite her doubts about her readiness for the exam, she is making an effort to try to write it.
6. The Siamese cat was rescued safely from the roof by a group of patient firefighters.
7. She found the election results pleasantly surprising and unexpected.
8. Do you think the rum in the punch is sufficient enough for this party?
9. After eating his usual supper of slops and table scraps, Wilbur was adequately satisfied.
10. Completely surrounded by insects, the picnickers surrendered their lunch and went to a restaurant instead.

The Sentence Simplified

When in doubt, take it out.

Anonymous

S ome fundamental understanding of the way a sentence is put together will help you analyze your style, eliminate grammatical errors, and punctuate more accurately. First, learn to differentiate the parts of a sentence.

When analyzing a sentence, always find the verb first. The verb is the part of the sentence that describes the action or the state of being.

Next, find the subject—ask WHO performed the action or WHAT is being described. Note that usually the subject appears before the verb.

Example

Elwy ripped his pants.

What is the verb? (ripped—an action) *Who* or *what* ripped his pants? (Elwy)

Her desk looks like a disaster area.

What is the verb? (looks—a state of being) *Who* or *what* looks like a disaster area? (Her desk)

The most common English sentence is made up of a subject, a verb, and an object, usually in that order.

Example

The child refused to eat her dinner.
   S   V   O

She threw her dish on the floor.
 S   V   O

She ignored her father's pleading.
 S   V   O

Children do not appreciate what their parents do for them.
  S   V   O

In each of these cases, the first noun or pronoun in the sentence is the subject, which performs the action. What follows the subject is the predicate, made up of the verb, which describes the action, and the object, which receives the action.

Another common simple sentence pattern is subject, verb, and complement. Here the verb must be a linking verb that describes a state of being, rather than an action.

Example

Elwy is not stupid.
 S V   C

He appears sluggish today.
S   V   C

He seems uninterested in everything around him.
S   V   C

He may be sleeping.
S   V   C

A sentence is a grammatical unit which can stand alone. It must be composed of a subject and verb and either an object or a complement.

■ Parts of Speech

A knowledge of the roles parts of speech play will help you understand how your sentences are constructed.

Nouns

Nouns name something: a person, place, or thing. They may be abstract or concrete. As a general rule, something may be classified as a noun if you can put an article ("a," "an," or "the") or a possessive pronoun ("my," "her") in front of it.

Example

girdle   ideology
suspenders   teacher
shoes   workmanship

Pronouns

Pronouns stand in the place of nouns. There are many kinds of pronouns.

Example

her husband (i.e. the husband of Alice)
everybody's business (i.e. the business of all citizens)
He ate **it**. (i.e. the spinach)
He disagreed with her views, all of **which** were feminist. (i.e. her views)

Verbs

A verb is an action word or a word which describes a state of being. It may have many forms and tenses. It also may be composed of an auxiliary verb and a main verb.

Example

Children **should not play** in the traffic.
Trespassers **will be prosecuted**.
I **am not going to take** it anymore.

Adjectives

Adjectives describe or modify nouns.

Example

loathesome	empirical
hungry	boring
cute	obvious

Adverbs

Adverbs describe or modify verbs, adjectives, and other adverbs. They often end in "ly."

Example

hungrily	very
dangerously	seldom
later	never

Prepositions

The preposition is a linking word that is always followed by a noun.

Example

over the hill	**on** the take
through the woods	**by** the sea
behind his back	**for** your information

Conjunctions

Conjunctions are used to join two words, phrases, or clauses.

Example

He sent valentines to Elizabeth **and** to Margaret.
After the examination, he went home to drown his sorrows.
Neither Mark **nor** Tracy won the race.

Interjections

Interjections are exclamatory words or phrases that interrupt a sentence.

Example

Yes, there is a Santa Claus.
Good heavens! Is this story true?

Common Sentence Problems

> Writing is hard work. A clear sentence is no accident.
>
> *William Zinsser*

A well-structured sentence tells its readers where to start and where to stop. The sentence, if it is correctly formed, constitutes a complete thought. It contains a main subject and a main verb connected to the subject.

■ Sentence Structure

Avoid fragments

A sentence fragment lacks either a subject or a main verb. Sometimes, it ignores the connection between them.

Example

X *She did not heed the mechanic's advice. But instead decided to ignore the noise coming from under the hood.* (missing subject: she)

✔ *She did not heed the mechanic's advice. Instead she decided to ignore the noise coming from under the hood.*

X *He had many hobbies. Watching sports, watching television, and watching old movies.* (no connection to the subject: he)

✔ *He had many hobbies: watching sports, watching television, and watching old movies.*

X *His vacation on the cruise ship was disappointing, since he missed his girlfriend. Plus the fact that he was always seasick.* (a subordinate clause with no connection to the main clause)

✔ *His vacation on the cruise ship was disappointing, since he missed his girlfriend, and he was always seasick.*

Note: A fragment may, on rare occasions, be used for rhetorical effect. Deliberate fragments must, however, be used sparingly. It is also a wise idea to use a dash (two hyphens in typing) before a deliberate sentence fragment to indicate its purpose to your reader.

Example

—*By no means.*

Avoid run-on sentences

A run-on sentence is actually two sentences which run together without any punctuation to indicate where one ends and the next begins.

Example

X *The bus is gone already it left ten minutes ago.*
✓ *The bus is gone already. It left ten minutes ago.*

Avoid comma splices

A comma splice is similar to a run-on sentence. It occurs when two main clauses are "spliced," or incorrectly joined, by a comma. The comma splice fails to show the relationship between two clauses.

Example

X *The rain will continue throughout the long weekend, the sunny weather will return on Tuesday.*

X *The $50 was only an estimate, the repairs will cost $500.*

A comma splice, like a visible seam, is a sign of faulty workmanship. There are several methods by which it may be corrected. Run-ons may also be treated the same way:

1. Join the two ideas with one of the following co-ordinating conjunctions: and, or, nor, for, but, yet, so.

Example

✓ *The rain will continue throughout the long weekend, but the sunny weather will return on Tuesday.*

✓ *The $50 was only an estimate, for the repairs will cost $500.*

2. Join the two ideas with a subordinating conjunction.

Example

✓ *Although the rain will continue throughout the long weekend, the sunny weather will return on Tuesday.*

✓ *Because the $50 was only an estimate, the repairs will cost $500.*

3. Form two separate sentences.

Example

✓ *The rain will continue throughout the long weekend. The sunny weather will return on Tuesday.*

✓ *The $50 was only an estimate. The repairs will cost $500.*

4. Join the two ideas with a semicolon.

Use this method of correction only if the two ideas in question are logically connected. Note that sometimes a word may be used as a conjunctive adverb to join two sentences with a semicolon. Words such as "however," "therefore," and "hence" frequently serve this function.

Example
***

✔ *The rain will continue throughout the long weekend; however, the sunny weather will return on Tuesday.*

✔ *The $50 was only an estimate; the repairs will cost $500.*

EXERCISE

Correct run-ons, fragments, and comma splices in the following sentences. Some may be correct as they stand.

1. Ethelbert sought revenge, his wife had given his clothes to the Salvation Army and left him without a stitch.
2. He won the award for best director, he thanked supporters and rivals alike, hoping to cover all the categories.
3. Making a will is a good idea, if you want to make sure that the right person is left with your debts.
4. Credit cards that allow you to buy luxuries on a whim.
5. She was intimidated by the answering machine, she lost her voice at the sound of the tone.
6. Dentists who use drills and ask complicated questions at the same time.
7. Mary began a support group for lazy people she believed that her idle friends needed somewhere to go in the evenings so they could relax.
8. Procrastination was my favourite hobby, until I found that it left me with too much spare time.
9. Having a baby means giving up privacy and free time, however it allows you to invest in the future.
10. A birthday present that reminds him of how much closer he is to retirement.

◼ Modifiers

Modifiers are descriptive words or phrases. A modifier may be a simple adverb or an adjective, or a more complex adverbial phrase or adjectival phrase. A modifier should describe clearly and unambiguously. To do so, it must be as near in the sentence as possible to the thing described.

Avoid misplaced modifiers

A modifier, whether a word or a phrase, should be placed next to the word it describes.

Example

X She sliced the cake using the knife.
✔ Using the knife, she sliced the cake.
X Picking lice out of each other's coats, the tourists observed the baboons.
✔ The tourists observed the baboons picking lice out of each other's coats.

Watch the position of limiting modifiers

A limiting modifier is a word which qualifies part or all of the statement. Consider carefully the placement of the following modifiers (and others): *only*, *just*, *nearly*, *almost*, *hardly*.

Example

a) Only David read the book. (No one else read it.)

b) David only read the book. (He did not make notes on it.)

c) David read the book only. (He did not read the accompanying reviews.)

Avoid squinting modifiers

A squinting modifier is ambiguously placed in the sentence, so that the writer's intention is unclear.

Example

The witness said later he discovered the body.

In this case, it is unclear which of the two possible meanings is intended:

a) The witness later said he discovered the body.
b) The witness said he discovered the body later.

Avoid dangling modifiers

A modifier dangles when what it is meant to describe is accidentally left out of the sentence.

Example

X After typing all night, the dog ate my research paper in the morning.
✔ After typing all night, I discovered in the morning that the dog had eaten my research paper.

OR

✔ After I had typed all night, the dog ate my research paper in the morning.

Dangling modifiers which end in "ing" are usually easy to spot. Remember, however, that a dangling modifier may also involve a prepositional phrase or an infinitive form. A dangling modifier may also occur at the end of a sentence.

Example

X As a pet owner, chihuahuas are more highly recommended than terriers.
✔ As a pet owner, I would recommend chihuahuas more highly than terriers.
X To make an omelet, some eggs must be broken.
✔ To make an omelet, you must break some eggs.
X Her medical bills were costly, being hospitalized without health insurance.
✔ Being hospitalized without health insurance, she found her medical bills were costly.

OR

✔ Since she was hospitalized without health insurance, her medical bills were costly.

Note that some modifiers apply to the entire sentence rather than to any one word or phrase within it. These constructions, called *absolute modifiers*, include phrases such as "To make a long story short" and "All things considered."

EXERCISE

Make corrections to the following sentences.

1. Chicken is eaten by many Canadian families, especially when roasted.
2. After hearing you talk to me that way, our wedding is cancelled.
3. Being a very sensitive person, rudeness offends me greatly.
4. Having broken his nose, the nurses took the patient to the emergency ward.
5. Students who criticize their teachers often may fail.
6. Snarling and showing his teeth, the zookeeper fed the lion his breakfast.
7. The fortune teller told me in August I would meet the man of my dreams.
8. I read that Nancy Reagan is suing her husband for divorce on grounds of adultery in the *National Enquirer*.
9. Her speech teacher took her to task about her careless attitude after being unprepared on three separate occasions.
10. Staggering from the bar after an evening of overindulgence, the sun was rising.

■ Pronoun Reference and Agreement

A pronoun, as the name suggests, acts *for* a noun, or in the place of a noun. A pronoun should almost always refer to a specific noun in the sentence itself. The noun to which it refers is called an *antecedent*. When a pronoun does not refer clearly to its antecedent, confusing or ambiguous writing is the result.

A guide to proper pronoun usage

Make sure your pronoun matches its antecedent. A pronoun must agree in gender: it may be masculine (he, him, his), feminine (she, her, hers), or neuter (it, it, its). A pronoun must also agree in number: it may be singular or plural.

In gender

Example

*Nancy named **her first child** Kyle.*
*Nancy named **him** Kyle.*

In the second sentence "her first child" has been replaced by the masculine pronoun "him."

In the past, the masculine pronouns ("he," "his," "him") were used to refer generally to nouns that were not specifically feminine.

Example

*The reader must consult his **own** taste.*

Although the masculine pronoun is still, strictly speaking, grammatically correct, many people now find its general use offensive. It is now more common to find a sentence like the following:

*The reader must consult **his** or **her** own taste.*

For those who find the use of "his or her" cumbersome, the best solution is to use the plural pronoun (and an accompanying plural noun, of course.)

Example

*Readers must consult **their** own tastes.*

The determination of gender in English does not pose much of a problem, apart from this dispute. Problems do arise, however, with the number of pronouns.

In number

1. Be sure to locate the correct antecedent for the pronoun in question.

Example

*Debbie is one of those women WHO **have chosen** to leave the job market to stay home with **their** children.*

"Women" [plural], because it is the noun closest to the relative pronoun, is the antecedent of the pronoun WHO; hence, both the verb "have chosen" and the pronoun "their" are plural.

*Debbie is the only one of her sisters WHO **has made** this choice.*

"One" [singular] is the antecedent of the pronoun WHO; hence, the verb "has made" is singular.

2. Be especially careful with collective nouns and their pronoun replacements.

When a collective noun is considered as a unit, the pronoun which stands for it is singular.

Example

*The Senate Review Board made **its** decision.*

Here the Board acts as a unit.

When the component parts of a collective noun are considered individually, the pronoun which stands for it is plural.

Example

*The Senate Review Board cast **their** votes.*

Here the Board acts individually; each member casts his or her separate vote.

3. Be careful of imprecise use of some indefinite pronouns.

Words like "anyone," "anybody," "someone," "somebody," "everyone," "everybody," "each," "either," "neither," "nobody," and "no one" are indefinite pronouns, all of which generally take singular verbs.

Example

Would anyone wishing to help please leave his or her name?

Ideally, "his or her" should follow an indefinite pronoun, if the construction is to avoid charges of sexism. In conversation, we would probably say,

Would anyone wishing to help please leave their name?

This form, despite its regular occurrence in spoken English, is still considered imprecise grammatically. It should properly be replaced by the following:

Would all those who wish to help please leave their names?

In case

Pronouns, besides being masculine or feminine, singular or plural, also have different forms depending on their case. They may be used as subjects ("he," "she," "they"), the objects ("him," "her," "them") or in the possessive ("his," "her," "their").

1. Use the subjective form if the pronoun is the subject of a verb (stated or implied).

Example

*The detective believed it was **she** (who had committed the crime).*

"She" is used here because a verb is implied.

*It was **he** who was responsible for the passing of the bill.*

"He" is used here because it functions as the subject of the verb "was."

This precision is essential in written English, but in informal speech, "It's me" or "It was her" are considered acceptable.

2. **Make sure to use the objective form of the pronoun if it is the object of a verb.**

   Example

   An angry customer sent Laura a letter.

   *An angry customer sent **her it**.*

In the second version, the objective forms for both pronouns—objects of the verb "sent"—have been substituted.

   *An angry customer sent Laura and **me** a letter.* (not "Laura and I")

In this example, if you remove the words "Laura and," the correct choice of pronoun becomes obvious.

3. **Make sure to use the objective form of the pronoun if it is the object of a preposition.**

   Example

   ***Between** you and me, I think you should use a spoon instead of a fork.*

   *He gave the lottery ticket **to** him and me.*

4. **After "than" or "as," use the form of the pronoun that would be used in the complete implied clause.**

   Example

   *The wrestler is more muscular than **he** [is].*

   *You can write as well as **she** [can].*

Note the difference in meaning in the following examples:

   I love you as much as he [does].

   I love you as much as him. [I love him.]

■ Pronoun Problems in Essay Writing

1. Use personal pronouns with discretion.

Too few personal references in an essay may be as awkward as too many. Few instructors disallow the use of "I" entirely. Its occasional use should prevent needless circumlocution and impersonality. Never stoop to cold and formal constructions like "It is the opinion of this writer," or the overly polite "myself." "We" may rarely be accepted, though its overuse may sound pompous. "One" may serve as an alternative, though it runs the risk of sounding too distanced and impersonal.

You are writing your paper; its words and thoughts are yours. Avoid "I" and "in my opinion" only when a personal perspective might make your point seem weak or merely a matter of personal idiosyncrasy.

2. Check to see that your pronoun references are present and accounted for.

UNCLEAR: *In big cities, they do not trust strangers.*
CLEARER: *Residents of big cities do not trust strangers.*

UNCLEAR: *She patted the dog's nose, and it bit her.*
CLEARER: *When she patted its nose, the dog bit her.*

UNCLEAR: *He sympathizes with the difficulties of management, although he has never been one.*
CLEARER: *Although he has never been a manager, he sympathizes with the difficulties of management.*

3. Avoid broad pronoun references.

A broad pronoun reference occurs when a word like "this," "which," or "that" is used to refer to an idea rather than to a specific word in the sentence. Some broad references may be tolerated, if the meaning is generally clear. Be careful of raising unanswered questions in the reader's mind, however.

UNCLEAR: *Darwin's* Origin of Species *caused considerable controversy at the time of its publication.* **This** *was a direct influence upon Tennyson's poetry.*

CLEARER: *Darwin's* Origin of Species *caused considerable controversy at the time of its publication.* **This book** *was a direct influence upon Tennyson's poetry.*

"This" does not clearly refer to any specific noun in the first sentence. The error can best be corrected by the simple addition of a word ("book") after "this" to clarify the author's point.

EXERCISE

Improve the usage of the pronouns in the following sentences.

1. Each of you must ask themselves if you want to wear a perfume made from the secretions of goat glands.
2. Before you and me become writers, we must decide who we should imitate: Violet Winspear or Leo Tolstoy.
3. "Between you and I," said the bankrupt socialite, "I really don't know where my next bottle of Grand Marnier will come from."
4. Peggy is one of those spunky women who intends to buy a motorcycle and a saxophone when her children are old enough to leave the nest.
5. Although my wife is better looking than me, this haircut suits both her and I.
6. Even if you didn't buy an exclusive membership, you don't need to be one to attend the jumble sale.
7. Professors have often ignored slow students, not caring if they complained about poor grades, but only if they covered all the material in their lectures.
8. If a customer is not satisfied with the fondue, they should complain to the waiter, and it will be taken back to the kitchen.
9. Murray sat down at the bar beside his friend and drank his beer.
10. Everything you suspect about we grammarians is true.

■ Subject and Verb Agreement

The subject and verb in a sentence are closely connected. In order for the sentence to express itself clearly, the subject and the verb must agree.

Most problems with agreement between subject and verb are caused by difficulties in locating the subject of a verb. Solve these problems by locating the verb in each clause. Remember first that a verb describes either an action or a state of being. Next, ask WHO or WHAT is performing that action or is being described. The answer to the questions WHO or WHAT is the subject of the verb. Having located the subject and verb, you may then check to see that they match.

Example

The boss wants to see you in his office.

WHO wants to see me?
—The boss. ("boss" is the subject of the verb "wants")

How to match subjects and verbs correctly

Check to see that verbs agree in number with their subjects. Singular subjects take singular verbs; plural subjects take plural verbs.

Problems to watch for:

1. **The noun which immediately precedes the verb may not be the subject.**

Example

Each one of us has already given at the office.

The correct subject is "one."

2. **Subjects joined by "and" are usually, but not always, plural.**

Example

My mentor and spiritual advisor is in trouble with the law.

"My mentor and spiritual advisor" refers to one person.

3. **Singular subjects that are joined by phrases other than "and" are not made plural. Such phrases as "as well as," "in addition to," and "along with" have no effect on the agreement of the verb.**

Example

An eraser, in addition to pencils and paper, is needed to calculate a tax return.

"In addition to pencils and paper" is not part of the subject.

4. **Subjects joined by "or" or "nor" are each considered separately. The verb agrees with the subject closest to it.**

   Example

   Neither love nor money motivates him.

   "Love" and "money" are each considered separately; hence, the verb is singular.

5. **The following subjects always take singular verbs: "each," "either," "neither," "one," and words ending in "body" or "one."**

   Example

   Neither of the courses has a final examination.

6. **Subjects like "some," "all," "most," "any," or "none" may take singular or plural verbs depending upon the noun they refer to.**

   Example

   *Some of the courses **have** a final examination.* (plural verb)

   *All of us **like** champagne.* (plural verb)

   *All of the champagne **is** finished.* (singular verb)

7. **A collective noun, used to refer to a group of people or things, takes a singular verb when the collective is considered as a unit and a plural verb when each member is considered individually.**

   Example

   Singular (considered a unit):

   The committee is conducting an investigation.

   Plural (considered as individuals within the group):

   The committee are voting on the new measure tomorrow.

8. **A linking verb (a verb describing a state of being) agrees with its subject and not with its predicate.**

   Example

   The only risk in education is falling grades.

   "Risk" is the subject; hence, "is" is the appropriate verb.

   OR

   Falling grades are the only risk in education.

In this example, "falling grades" is the subject; hence, the plural verb is required.

9. **A verb still agrees with its subject, even when their order is inverted. The subject follows "there is" or "there are," "here is" or "here are," and the verb is singular or plural accordingly.**

Example

There are no other dangers to speak of.

Here "dangers" is the subject; hence, the correct verb is "are."

10. **Relative pronouns (who, which, that), acting as subjects, take singular or plural verbs depending on the words to which they refer (their antecedents).**

Example

Peppy is one of those unfortunate dogs that like to chase skunks.

"Dogs," the antecedent of "that," is plural; hence, the verb "like" is also plural.

BUT NOTE:

Peppy is the only one of these dogs that bathes regularly.

"One" is the antecedent in this case; hence, the verb "bathes" is singular.

11. **Some nouns may look plural though they are actually singular. Examples include "physics," "economics," "ethics," "news." Check doubtful usage in a dictionary.**

Example

Ethics is an important branch of philosophical thinking.

BUT NOTE:

The ethics of the radical group were called into question by the press.

EXERCISE

Correct the alignments between subject and verb in the following sentences.

1. Although Ken and Barbie are officially engaged, neither of them are anatomically correct.
2. The engineering student, as well as some of his fellow undergraduates, were arrested after putting a Mickey Mouse face on the university clock tower.
3. The rate of examination failures steadily increase during the hockey playoffs.
4. George is the only one of his friends who are invited to the party celebrating the achievements of the best and brightest.
5. At his heels was Nelson, a friendly Airedale terrier, and Silverbell, an aged but pretty cat.

6. When the poor woman bought a ticket to the ballet, her main worry were electrical storms which might cause a blackout and lead to the cancellation of the performance without the possibility of a refund.
7. In these days of rising divorce rates, both a fiftieth-anniversary card and a twenty-fifth anniversary card is needed to commemorate seventy-five years of matrimony.
8. At the city zoo, an animal such as a zebra, a monkey, or a giraffe eat better than the tourists who visit each day.
9. The main criteria of excellence in grammar is accuracy and fluency.

■ End Punctuation

1. Use a period after a statement, an indirect question, or a command.

Example

You'll be sorry. (statement)

Take the money and run. (command)

She asked me who performed my face lift. (indirect question)

2. Use a period after most abbreviations, except for common acronyms.

Example

Mr.	*CBC*
Ms.	*VCR*
Dr.	*CD player*

3. Use a question mark after a direct question.

Example

What were the causes of the War of 1812?

What is your favourite colour?

4. Use exclamation marks sparingly to express emphasis, and only in an informal essay. Use them in a formal essay at your own risk.

Example

X *The member of parliament denied the allegation!*
✔ *Surprisingly, the member of parliament denied the allegation.*

■ The Comma (,)

A comma is a light mark of punctuation. Some basic rules that govern its use are listed below. When in doubt about a particular usage, let clarity be your guide.

1. Use a comma before "and," "or," "nor," "for," "but," "yet," "so," if any of these words are used to join two independent clauses.

Example

I don't normally gush, but I'll make an exception in your case.

BUT NOTE:

A comma should not be used if a complete independent clause does not follow.

Example

Margaret does not watch television but instead prefers old-fashioned fun.

In this case, "but" actually joins a compound verb, rather than two independent clauses.

2. **Use a comma after a phrase or clause used to introduce the main subject and verb, unless the introductory element is very short.**

Example

Her voice quivering slightly, the red-haired girl rejected Charlie.

Unlike movie stars, swans mate for life.

Mrs. Robinson, we're going to have to stop meeting like this.

3. **Use a comma for the sake of contrast before an antithetical element.**

Example

He had hoped that his girlfriend would come alone, rather than with her German Shepherd.

I love you for your personality, not for your portfolio of stocks and bonds.

4. **Use a comma after a word or phrase that modifies an entire sentence.**

Example

Generally, grammar books are dull.

All things considered, I would advise you to leave while you still have the chance.

5. **Use commas to separate elements in a series.**

Example

Dorothy, the Scarecrow, and the Tin Woodsman join hands when confronted with the possible dangers of lions, tigers, and bears.

A comma before "and" at the end of the list is usually advisable to prevent confusion.

He came directly home from work, he kissed his wife at the door, and he went straight to bed.

Here commas are used to separate a series of independent clauses.

6. **Put commas around words, phrases, or clauses that interrupt a sentence. Commas may be used around a word or a group of words if that part of the sentence might be removed and still leave a subject and predicate.**

   ### Example

   His joking manner, although well-meant, was unappreciated.

   He was, however, not hired by the funeral director.

7. **Put commas around appositives, words that refer back to those that precede them.**

   ### Example

   Pierre Trudeau, the former prime minister, retired from public life in 1984.

   Fred, Melissa's pet gerbil, had an injured tail.

   In the above examples, "the former prime minister" and "Pierre Trudeau" are in apposition, as are "Melissa's pet gerbil" and "Fred."

8. **Put commas around interrupting phrases or clauses that are non-restrictive in meaning.**

   ### Example

   The squealing child, affectionately called King David the Terrible by his doting mother, was carried from the conference room.

   If the pair of commas and what they contain were removed, what remains is still a perfectly good sentence. A pair of commas, like parentheses, is used to enclose incidental information.

9. **Commas should not enclose material that is restrictive, that is, essential to the sentence's meaning.**

   ### Example

   X   *Girls, who just want to have fun, should be careful.*

   This statement suggests that all girls should be careful, rather than just the particular girls identified by the modifier.

   ✔   *Girls who just want to have fun should be careful.*

   This statement identifies which girls should be careful. The modifier, because it performs the necessary function of identification or limitation, cannot be surrounded by commas.

10. **Commas should not separate main sentence elements. Do not use a comma between a subject and verb or between a verb and an object or complement.**

> X *To err, is human.*
> ✔ *To err is human.*

"To err" is the subject and must not be separated from the verb "is."

> X *The only excuse for such bad behaviour, is ignorance.*
> ✔ *The only excuse for such bad behaviour is ignorance.*

"Ignorance" is the complement of the verb "is" and must not be separated from it.

EXERCISE

Add commas where needed in the following sentences.

1. Janice a delicate sensitive young woman explained to the academic counsellor that her life-long ambition was to become a prison warden.
2. Aunt Florence locked in the washroom at the Museum of Modern Art began to panic but luckily the janitor overheard her cries and came to her rescue.
3. He dreaded becoming a father since he feared responsibility diaper changes early-morning feedings and the possibility that his children would one day sue him for mental cruelty.
4. The retiring professor made the following solemn vow at the party held in his honour: "I'll lie steal cheat or kill but I'll never mark a paper again."
5. But really Michael I thought you liked me.
6. Woody Allen a brilliant and innovative director has recorded many of the trials traumas and triumphs of his personal life on videocassettes now available at the corner store.
7. The ailing eccentric purchased fresh flowers each week for he relished the idea of being able to outlive them.
8. I do not approve of your new suit however fetching you think it may be nor do I generally like colours not found in nature.
9. Although he had specifically asked for a crystal ball for his birthday he was disappointed to discover that it did not come with instructions.
10. Guard against excessive openmindedness or you may be told that some of your liberal ideas are falling out of the holes in your head.

■ The Colon (:)

The colon is used to introduce something.

Remember the following rules for colon usage:

1. Use a colon only after a complete sentence (that is, after an independent clause).

Example

> X *He sat in the front row because: he wanted to look keen, and he wanted to be the first one out of the classroom.*
> ✔ *He sat in the front row for two reasons: he wanted to look keen, and he wanted to be the first one out of the classroom.*

2. **Use a colon after a complete sentence to introduce ideas, lists, or quotations.**

Example

The audience greeted him with one unanimous reaction: they hissed.

Their charm school was designed to teach three essential things: how to befriend people you don't really like, how to act as if you are independently wealthy, and how to get prestigious jobs for which you are not really qualified.

■ The Semicolon (;)

A semicolon is a heavier punctuation mark than a comma, but lighter than a period. In general, use a semicolon only where you might use a period instead.

Semicolons are especially useful in the following cases:

1. **Use a semicolon to join two closely related main clauses.**

The use of a semicolon instead of a coordinating conjunction shows a close connection (or a sharp antithesis) between two ideas.

Example

Love inspires sacrifice; friendship accepts compromise.

2. **Use a semicolon with a transitional word or phrase, when it is used to join two main clauses.**

Transitional words or phrases such as "however," "moreover," "furthermore," "hence," "as a result," and "consequently" (and others) may be used in this way.

Example

I do love you; however, I do not like your mother.

The semicolon takes the place of a period in this sentence.

BUT NOTE:

I do, however, love you.

In this case, "however" is not used to join two main clauses. Since it interrupts one main clause, commas are adequate punctuation.

3. **Use a semicolon to separate items listed in a series, if commas are already used as internal punctuation.**

Example

She refused to marry him for three reasons: one, he was not wealthy enough; two, he was not handsome enough; and three, he was just not her type.

EXERCISE

Add or substitute colons or semicolons in the following sentences, keeping in mind that some may be correct as they stand.

1. Alfred Hitchcock did not use real blood in the shower scene of *Psycho* Janet Leigh is dripping in chocolate syrup.
2. Losing weight is easy if you keep these rules in mind exercise regularly, consume fewer calories, and keep the refrigerator door closed firmly.
3. Brian Costello advised me to invest in a Registered Retirement Savings Plan however I do not expect to retire unless I find a job first.
4. The seven deadly sins to which he was most prone included lust, sloth, and avarice.
5. A computer has all the attributes of an obedient slave it works uncomplainingly, asks nothing for itself, and doesn't talk back when you use it badly.
6. The hostess couldn't decide which couples to invite to her birthday soiree Phil and Marlo, Steve and Eydie, or Madonna and Sean.
7. The woman working in the pet store was perfect for the job she owned three cats Larry, a Siamese Curly, a long-haired Persian Mo, a tortoise-shell with a nasty disposition, and Fathead, a hamster.
8. The teacher recommended however that the students not purchase their term papers, but that they write them instead.
9. Lester forgot his books at school consequently he was free to watch all-star wrestling on Saturday afternoon.
10. She really did not want to accompany Alastair to the roller derby besides she had to wash her hair.

■ The Dash

Type a dash using two hyphens, with no spaces before or after.

Example

They wished each other well--but not too well.

1. Use a dash for emphasis around parenthetical expressions.

Example

Her fur coat—though it was a cheap synthetic—made her feel rich and pampered.

Note that commas are also correct in this sentence but less emphatic.

2. Use a dash to introduce something with extra emphasis.

Example

An exciting evening for him meant two things—reading wildlife magazines and watching Knowlton Nash.

Note that a colon is also correct in this sentence but less emphatic.

3. Keep the dash in reserve for special occasions. Use it sparingly, especially in formal writing.

■ Parentheses

Parentheses are used to enclose incidental material. They (or the words they enclose) serve the same function as an aside in a theatrical production. Though they get the reader's attention, the material they enclose is presented as "inside information."

1. **Use parentheses in formal writing to enclose the necessary definition of a term at its first appearance.**

   ### *Example*

   The VCR (video cassette recorder) can be used to screen home movies as well as rented ones, if you own a video camera.

2. **Use parentheses to enclose any part of a sentence that might be enclosed by commas or dashes, if the reader has only passing interest in it.**

   ### *Example*

   The sex therapist (on her weekly talk show) encourages people to share their fantasies with viewers across the nation.

3. **Use parentheses sparingly. Too many make the writing self-conscious and hard to follow.**

   ### *Example*

   X It is my view (after considering all the available sources) that the American space program should be halted.

■ Possession

Apostrophes are used after nouns and indefinite pronouns (e.g. "anyone," "somebody") to indicate possession. Note these general rules:

1. **Add "'s" to form the possessive case if the owner is singular.**

   ### *Example*

   "sow's ear"—the ear of the sow
   "cat's pyjamas"—the pyjamas of the cat
   "baby's bottom"—the bottom of the baby

   Note that even when the word ends in "s," the ending is usually "'s," since that is how we pronounce it.

   ### *Example*

   "Keats's poetry"—the poetry of Keats
   "Dickens's novels"—the novels of Dickens

2. **Add "s'" to form the possessive case if the owners are plural.**

Example

"students' newspaper"—the newspaper of the students
"teachers' association"—the association of the teachers

Words that do not form the plural with "s" are made possessive by the addition of "'s."

Example

"the children's hour"—the hour of the children
"women's liberation"—the liberation of women
"the geese's eggs"—the eggs of the geese

3. **Do not use an apostrophe with possessive pronouns.**

Example

The corn flakes are theirs. The potato chips are hers. The chocolate chip cookies are mine. The rest of the groceries are yours.

Note that "its" (another possessive pronoun) also does *not* have an apostrophe. Do not confuse the possessive pronoun "its" with the contraction for "it is" (it's).

Example

It's raining. (It is raining.)

Its bottle empty, the baby howled with hunger. (possessive)

EXERCISE

Correct the following sentences by adding apostrophes where necessary.

1. According to the fortune tellers prediction, the errors of your past years will not affect tomorrows plans.
2. Wendys daughter, who will be thirteen next month, has started shopping in the womens lingerie department.
3. Ross sportscar has many extras, but its hood ornament needs to be replaced.
4. For your healths sake, you should quit smoking, lose a few pounds, and stop blackmailing your former employer.
5. The Beatles new compact discs include *Help!*, *Please Please Me*, *Rubber Soul*, *A Hard Days Night*, *Beatles for Sale*, and *Revolver*.
6. The joggers tracksuit was remarkable for its bright colour and its loose fit.
7. Travellers cheques and shoppers credit cards will not be honoured when the store celebrates its fiftieth anniversary.
8. Yesterdays chaperone is todays cruise director.
9. Evita Peron is the unlikely heroine of Andrew Lloyd Webber and Tim Rices Broadway musical, *Evita*.
10. The waiters and waitresses gratuities were included in the foods basic cost.

Documenting—MLA and APA Guidelines

Your bibliography should list all items that you quote, paraphrase, or use as source material. Two basic styles of documentation will be covered in this section: that of the *MLA Handbook*, most commonly used in the humanities, and that of the APA publication manual, often used in the social sciences.

■ Sample Bibliographical Entries in MLA Style

The examples which follow show how certain entries would appear in a bibliography, if you follow the guidelines of the Modern Language Association. These entries should serve as models when you prepare your own bibliography page. In MLA style, this page is called "Works Cited." If you need further information, consult: Gibaldi, Joseph, and Walter S. Achtert. *MLA Handbook for Writers of Research Papers*. 2nd ed. New York: Modern Language Association, 1984.

Books

One author

Frazer, James George. The Golden Bough: A Study in Magic
     and Religion. New York: Macmillan, 1922.

Use a shortened version of the publisher's name (in this case, Macmillan Publishing Company), making sure that your label is still recognizable. Include complete subtitles in bibliographical entries, and underline title and subtitle continuously.

Two authors and edition after the first

Strunk, William, Jr., and E. B. White. The Elements of
     Style. 3rd ed. New York: Macmillan, 1979.

Three authors

Bercuson, David, J. L. Granatstein, and W. R. Young.
     Sacred Trust? Brian Mulroney and the Conservative
     Party in Power. Toronto: Doubleday, 1986.

More than three authors

Cornell, Paul G., et al. Canada: Unity in Diversity.
     Toronto: Holt, 1967.

Corporate author

Imperial Oil Limited. <u>The Review</u>. Toronto: Imperial Oil,
    Spring 1987.

Editor

Drabble, Margaret, ed. <u>The Oxford Companion to English
    Literature</u>. 5th ed. Oxford: Oxford UP, 1985.

Government publication

Canada. Minister of Supply and Services Canada. <u>Canada
    Year Book 1985</u>. Ottawa: Statistics Canada, 1985.

Story or article from an anthology

Ludwig, Jack. "The Calgary Stampede." <u>Active Voice: An
    Anthology of Canadian, American and Commonwealth
    Prose</u>. Eds. W. H. New and W. E. Messenger.
    Scarborough: Prentice-Hall, 1980. 111-20.

Translation

Ringuet. <u>Thirty Acres</u>. Trans. Felix and Dorothea Walker.
    Toronto: McClelland, 1960.

Reprint

Montgomery, L. M. <u>Anne of Green Gables</u>. 1908. Toronto:
    McGraw-Hill, 1968.

The original hardcover edition was published in 1908. The paperback version
appeared in 1968.

A work in more than one volume

Rollins, Hyder Edward, ed. <u>The Letters of John Keats: 1814-
    1821</u>. 2 vols. Cambridge: Harvard UP, 1958.

A work in a series

Woodman, Ross. <u>James Reaney</u>. Canadian Writers New Canadian
    Library 12. Toronto: McClelland, 1971.

The volume number is given in Arabic numerals and without the abbreviation
vol.

Magazines, newspapers, and journals

Unsigned article

"Students again face tight housing market." <u>The London
    Free Press</u> 16 Aug. 1986: C2.

The names of months other than May, June, and July are usually abbreviated.
"C2" refers to the section and page number of the newspaper.

Daily newspaper

Matyas, Joe. "Grandmother new church moderator". <u>The
    London Free Press</u> 16 Aug. 1986: A1.

When not part of the newspaper's name, the city's name should be given in brackets after the title.

Weekly magazine or newspaper
Steacy, Anne, and Ben Barber. "Losing the race against drug dealers." Maclean's 18 Aug. 1986: 46.

Monthly or bi-monthly magazine
Brown, Andrew. "The Freedom Portfolio." Your Money May-June 1986: 61-62.

Journal—continuous pagination through the year
Campbell, Jane. " 'Competing Towers of Babel': Some Patterns of Language in Hard Times." English Studies in Canada 10.4 (1984): 416-35.

When the pages of a journal are numbered consecutively through the year, a comma precedes the page reference. Note also that an issue number ("4" in this case) follows the volume number "10." They are separated by a period.

Journal—separate pagination for each issue
Little, Jean. "A long distance friendship." Canadian Children's Literature 34 (1984): 23-30.

When the pages of a journal are numbered separately for each issue, a colon precedes the page reference.

Editorial
"Considering Refugees." Editorial. The Globe and Mail 7 May 1987: A6.

Book review
Miller, J. R. Rev. of The Man from Halifax: Sir John Thompson, Prime Minister, by P. B. Waite. Queen's Quarterly 93 (1986): 646-48.

Encyclopedia

Signed with name or initials
So[utham], B[rian] C. "Austen, Jane." Encyclopaedia Britannica: Macropaedia. 1974 ed.

This article appears with the initials B.C. So. appended to it. To identify it, you need only check the index of the encyclopedia and enclose the added information in brackets.

Unsigned
"Canadian Football League." Encyclopaedia Britannica: Micropaedia. 1974 ed.

Pamphlets, bulletins, and reports
Canada. Veterans Affairs Canada. A Day of Remembrance. Ottawa: Canadian Government, 1984.

Unpublished dissertations

DuBroy, Michael Thomas. "The Tale of the Folk: Revolution
   and the Late Prose Romances of William Morris." Diss.
   U of Western Ontario, 1982.

Micropublications

Books or periodicals in microprint form are documented as they would be in
their original form.

Non-print sources

Motion picture

My Financial Career. National Film Board. 1962.

Television or radio program

"Family and Survival." Phil Donahue Examines The Human
   Animal. NBC. WICU, Erie, PA. 15 Aug. 1986.

Television interview

Burgess, Anthony. Interview by Daniel Richler. The
   Journal. CBC-CFPL, London. 13 Apr. 1987.

Performance of stage play

Pericles. By William Shakespeare. Stratford Festival
   Theatre. Stratford. 6 July 1986.

Recording

Kunzel, Erich. Kunzel on Broadway: Erich Kunzel
   Conducting the Winnipeg Symphony Orchestra. Fanfare,
   DFL-9017, Toronto, 1985.

Lecture

Gedalof, Allan. "Mystery Writing." U.W.O. Senior Alumni
   Series. Wesanne McKellar Room, U of Western Ontario,
   London, Ontario. 14 Apr. 1987.

Interview

Wiseman, Adele. Personal Interview. 15 Apr. 1987.

For samples of citations of other non-print sources—games, globes, filmstrips,
microscope slides, and transparencies—consult Eugene B. Fleischer's *A Style
Manual for Citing Microform and Nonprint Media* (Chicago: American Library
Association, 1978).

■ Citing Sources in MLA Style

Whenever you refer to material from another source, whether book, journal
article, motion picture, or recording, you must acknowledge your source. Citing
your sources no longer necessitates footnotes or endnotes. Instead, citations of
sources are placed in the body of the essay in parentheses. A footnote or

endnote is only necessary if you have supplementary material to explain that does not properly belong in the text of the essay itself.

Simple citation

Include in parentheses after the citation only what is essential to guide the reader to the correct entry in the list of "Works Cited." Often, all that will be needed is the last name of the author followed by a page number. For example, if you were quoting from Margaret Laurence's *The Diviners*, the citation in the text would look like this:

> *Morag's collection of photographs gives the reader insight into her own hidden past. As she says, "I keep the snapshots not for what they show but for what is hidden in them" (Laurence 6).*

This citation refers the reader to the following entry on the "Works Cited" page:

> *Laurence, Margaret. The Diviners. Toronto: Bantam, 1974.*

If this is the only entry listed under Laurence, there is no confusion, and the reader knows that the quotation can be found on page 6 of the listed text.

Citation of more than one work by the same author

If, on the other hand, there are references to two works by the same author, a more distinct notation is required. Say that you referred in the same essay to Margaret Laurence's earlier novel, *A Jest of God*. You might, perhaps, make the following reference:

> *Rachel discovers her own capacity to hide the truth from herself. As she explains, "There is room enough in anyone's bonehouse for too much duplicity" (Laurence Jest 182).*

This reference makes it clear that there is more than one book by Laurence in the bibliography.

Citation of a work in more than one volume

If, in an essay about Keats's poetry, you decide to quote from the two-volume collection of Keats's letters, the citation would read as follows:

> *Keats, in the composition of the odes, dedicates himself to the search for "the true voice of feeling" (Letters 2:167).*

Here the Arabic numeral 2 refers to the second volume of the letters. A colon is used to separate the volume number from the page number.

Similar adjustments must be made to clarify abbreviated citations. Always remember to ask yourself what the reader needs to know in order to find the reference easily.

Citation of poetry and of long or short quotations

Avoid redundant citations. If the body of your essay already explains the source adequately, do not restate the information in parentheses. For example, you might write the following analysis of Keats's poetry:

> The poet speaks of the lure of death in "Ode to a Nightingale":
>
>> Darkling I listen; and, for many a time
>> I have been half in love with easeful Death,
>> Call'd him soft names in many a mused rhyme,
>> To take into the air my quiet breath. (51–54)

Here only the line numbers are listed in parentheses, since the title of the poem is given in the body of the essay itself. Note, too, that a long quotation is indented and written without quotation marks. Because the quoted matter is poetry, the lines are given as they are in the text. If the quotation was only two lines long, it would be written in the body of the essay in the following way, using quotation marks:

> The poet speaks of the lure of death in "Ode to a Nightingale": "Darkling I listen; and, for many a time /I have been half in love with easeful Death" (51–52).

Citation of poetic drama

A reference to a play must refer to act, scene, and line numbers, as in the following case:

> In Shakespeare's A Midsummer Night's Dream, Titania, enchanted with Bottom, sees the world around with romantic eyes. As she says,
>
>> The moon methinks looks with a watery eye;
>> And when she weeps, weeps every little flower,
>> Lamenting some enforced chastity. (3.1.202–04)

Punctuation of citations

Note that for citations within the text, punctuation appears *after* the parentheses. In quotations set off from the text, citations *follow* the final punctuation. To make citations as unobtrusive as possible, try to place them at the end, rather than in the middle, of sentences.

■ Sample Bibliographic Entries in APA Style

The following entries are arranged according to the style of the *Publication Manual of the American Psychological Association*. In this case, the bibliography is given the heading, "References." For further details on this style of documentation, consult: American Psychological Association. *Publication Manual of the American Psychological Association*. 3rd ed. Washington: American Psychological Assn., 1983.

Books
One author
Selye, H. (1956). <u>The Stress of Life</u>. New York: McGraw Hill.

Two authors

Gatchel, R. and Baum, A. (1983). <u>An Introduction to Health Psychology</u>. Reading, Massachusetts: Addison- Wesley.

Journals
One author

Turner, J. (1981). Social Support as a Contingency in Psychological Well-Being. <u>Journal of Health and Social Behavior</u>, <u>22</u>, 357-67.

Multiple authors

Turner, J., Frankel, G., & Levin, D. (1983). Social Support: Conceptualization, Measurement, and Implications for Mental Health. <u>Research in Community and Mental Health</u>, <u>3</u>, 67-111.

■ Citing Sources in APA Style

As with the MLA style of documentation, you may cite your sources in parentheses in APA style. In APA style, however, the year of publication is given with the author's last name; hence, the title of a work is never needed. Note details in the following examples:

Short Quotation

Social support is defined as "those relationships among people that provide not only material help and emotional assurance, but also the sense that one is a continuing object of concern on the part of other people" (Pilsuk, 1982, p. 20).

Long Quotation

Seligman (1975) argues that helplessness may lead to depression:

> *Those people who are particularly susceptible to depression may have had lives relatively devoid of mastery; their lives may have been full of situations in which they were helpless to influence the sources of suffering and relief. (p. 104)*

Note that, in this passage, the author's last name and the date of publication are not included in parentheses because they are already given in the body of the essay.

Paraphrase

Cobb (1976) insists that stress, not social support, is the key to understanding changes in health. Social support only acts as a buffer (p. 304).

Following these basic guidelines should help you assemble your notes and your bibliography with relative ease. Remember these guidelines as you prepare the documentation for your essay:

1. Be consistent.
2. Give your reader all the information needed to find a reference.
3. Check the sample research essay in this guide for a model of MLA format.
4. Check the appropriate style guide for further details.

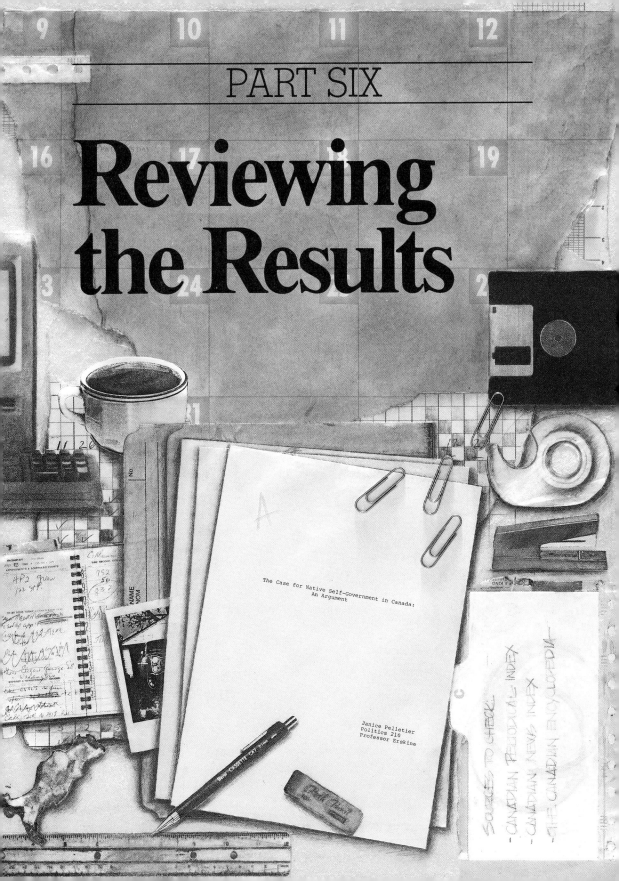

Perfecting the Essay

A poet can survive everything but a misprint.
Oscar Wilde

Even after all your hard work, some minor but significant detail may affect the reader's perception of your paper. Often these errors are the most embarrassing ones, errors which undercut your effort and distract the reader's attention from the elegance of your essay's form and the substance of its content. Like the emperor with no clothes, you and your work may be easily subjected to ridicule or to charges of arrogance if you neglect responsible proofreading and stringent self-criticism. To ensure the quality of your work, follow these steps:

1. Reflect on your image.

Just as you wouldn't buy an item of clothing without first looking to see if it suited you and fit properly, don't write a paper and then submit it without first assessing its immediate impact on its readers. Reread the paper, scrutinizing its details very carefully—preferably a few days after you have written it. Reading aloud will help you find any awkward instances of grammatical construction and style. If you *still* feel insecure, ask a friend to read it too.

2. If you can't be perfect, be careful.

Some errors, in this imperfect world, may still creep in. Make necessary corrections as unobtrusively as possible. Resist the impulse to retype the whole paper (possibly introducing new errors) and instead make the corrections neatly in black ink—above the line. Stroke out unwanted letters with a small vertical line and remove repeated words by the judicious use of "white-out" (liquid paper) or the simple horizontal stroke of a pen.

3. Make your paper "easy on the eyes."

Don't allow your essay to offend the eye. Specifically, avoid erasable bond paper (which baffles the instructor who tries to write on it). Avoid typewriter ribbon so faded that you develop eyestrain trying to read a paper typed with it. Make your handwriting bold, large, and neat. If you submit a computer printout, take special care in proofreading to avoid errors that may have been introduced in production. Submit the paper in a tidy folder, neatly stapled or paper clipped (as your instructor may prefer). Even if neatness is not an acknowledged criterion of excellence, there is no question that first impressions have a lasting effect.

4. Tie up any loose threads.

Don't submit your paper without checking such details as page numbers, exact quotations, bibliographical information, doubtful spellings, word divisions, and grammatical constructions.

5. Follow the "dress code."

Make sure that your assignment adheres to any conditions explicitly stated by the instructor, however arbitrary or trivial such matters may seem to you. Check to see that the mechanical format of your paper conforms to the expected standards of the instructor. Such items as the treatment of abbreviations, bibliographical arrangement, even the format of the title page and the position and form of page numbers need careful attention. Although you may have already invested considerable time in these matters, a last-minute check is a good idea.

Mending the Essay

> I think there is a demon who seats himself on the feather of my pen when I begin to write, and leads it astray from the purpose.
>
> *Sir Walter Scott*

I
f, when you get an essay back, you find that a similar demon seems to have led your work astray, there are still some things you can do to redeem it. It may be too late to get the kind of grade that you had in mind on this particular paper, but some of the tactics proposed below ought to make the next essay better.

First, don't throw the paper away in a fit of glee or gloom. You write essays not only to get grades but to learn how to write. Long after you have forgotten the facts and figures involved in writing your paper, you will still have the writing skills that were developed in its preparation. Your reading, writing, and research skills are the most visible parts of your education long after you graduate.

■ Deciphering Comments

1. Read the grader's comments when your essays are returned to you—regardless of the grade you receive.

Don't read only the comments accompanying the grade at the end of the paper, but also any questions or hints dropped in the margins or within the text of the paper.

2. Next, see that you understand what the comments and questions mean.

The list below should help:

agr	*—error in agreement (subject/verb or pronoun)*
awk	*— awkward wording*
case	*— error in pronoun case*
cs	*— comma splice*
D	*— diction*

dm	— dangling modifier
doc	— error in documentation
frag	— sentence fragment
gr	— grammar or usage
mm	— misplaced modifier
p	— error in punctuation
par	— problem with paragraphing
pass	— overuse of the passive voice
ref	— problem with pronoun reference
rep	— repetition
run-on	— run-on sentence
shift	— shift in verb tense or logic
sp	— spelling error
T	— error in verb tense
TS	— problem with thesis statement
trans	— transition
‖	— faulty parallelism
⌃	— something missing
wdy	— problem with wordiness

3. **Ask your instructor to explain a particular comment.**

4. **When you have read through the comments, try to analyze the kind of mistakes that you make most frequently and determine that you will take steps to eliminate them.**

5. **Next, consult a reliable guide in order to correct your mistakes.**

Such guides include a dictionary (for spelling errors and errors of usage), a writing/grammar handbook (such as this one), or a guide to proper format of notes and bibliography (such as the *MLA Handbook*).

■ Learning from Experience

1. Analyze the strengths and weaknesses of your style.

At first, this may seem a puzzling endeavour, but after a time you should be able to discern changes in your writing—not only in its mechanics, but in the development of its thought as well.

2. Analyze your writing habits.

Do you find that you have certain favourite expressions that crop up too often? Do your readers frequently comment that your sentences are too complex or too simple? Do certain tactics in your argument often meet with an unfavourable response? Paying attention to these trends in your collected essays will enable you to become more sensitive to your patterns of self-expression and more able to prevent problems in the future.

3. Keep a list of your most common spelling and grammar errors from past work.

Refer to this list when you are about to write the final draft of your next paper. It may help eliminate some pitfalls.

4. Exercise your writing skills.

Reading is probably not a strong enough remedy to cure you of some errors; writing is the recommended therapy. If possible, set yourself the task of completing some exercises aimed at a specific problem diagnosed by your instructor. If, for example, dangling modifiers are a persistent problem, consult the section in this book on their diagnosis and treatment. Your instructor may agree to check your answers afterwards.

5. Rewrite.

Rewriting is also a good way of curing some of the ills of essay writing. Try, for example, to recast a troublesome paragraph in a clearer, smoother prose, incorporating your instructor's suggestions. Remember though that no writer ever developed a style mechanically; it is intimately related to thought. Rethink your thoughts as you rewrite. You will learn a great deal about the impact your writing has on its readers if you remember the grader's comments.

6. Work through appropriate sections of this book with an essay that has just been returned.

This exercise will help you in your next essay assignment.

7. Experiment.

Writing should not always be a chore. Sometimes, when you find yourself able to express something exactly the way you want to, writing becomes play. Allow yourself to become comfortable as you write. Remember that your real writing purpose, grades and completed assignments aside, is to say what you want to say. Practice will make writing a satisfying form of self-expression.

Glossary of Usage

This glossary lists some words that are a common source of errors, either because they are confused with other words, or because they are not acceptable in standard usage. Check through this list if you are in doubt about a particular usage.

accept/except
"Accept" is a verb that means to "approve"; "except" is a verb or a preposition that means "to exclude."

> I would **accept** your proposition **except** for my husband and six children.

advice/advise
"Advice" is a noun; "advise" is a verb.

> I **advise** you to follow your mother's **advice**.

affect/effect
"Affect" is usually a verb; "effect" is usually a noun. Note, however, that "effect" may occasionally be a verb, meaning "to bring about."

> His break-up with his girlfriend **affected** his grade point average.

> A broken heart may have a bad **effect** on scholastic achievement.

> He thought perhaps that by writing a tear-stained letter he could **effect** a reconciliation.

allude/elude
"To allude" means "to make indirect reference to"; "to elude" means "to escape."

> A lewd reference may **elude** you, but it may perhaps **allude** to another literary source.

allusion/illusion
The first is a veiled or indirect reference; the second is a deception.

> She found the poet's **allusion** to Shakespeare; her belief that the words came from Milton was an **illusion**.

a lot/allot
"A lot" is a colloquialism for "many" or "a great deal"; "to allot" is a verb, meaning "to divide" or "to parcel out."

> Each of the heiresses had been **allotted a lot** of their grandfather's fortune.

all together/altogether
The first means "in a group"; the second means "completely" or "entirely."

> **All together**, the students in the class decided that the teacher was **altogether** incompetent.

all right/alright

The *first* is the correct spelling.

among/between

"Among" involves more than two; "between" involves just two.

> **Among** *his peers he is considered a genius;* **between** *you and me, I think he is overrated.*

amount of/number of

"Amount of" is for quantities that cannot be counted and hence is followed by a singular noun; "a number of" is for quantities that may be counted and takes a plural noun.

> *A* **number** *of students drink large* **amounts** *of alcohol.*

as/because

"Because" should be used instead of "as" in a sentence meant to show cause-and-effect, since "as" or "while" may also refer to the passage of time.

> X **As** *he was awaiting trial, he refused to speak to the press.* (ambiguous)
> ✔ **Because** *he was awaiting trial, he refused to speak to the press.*

aspect

Avoid this vague word.

being/being as/being that

"Being" can almost always be eliminated. "Being as" or "being that" should be replaced by "because" or "since."

bottom line

This popular bit of financial jargon has no place in formal writing.

can/may

"Can" implies ability; "may" implies permission or possibility.

> *I* **may** *go shopping today, since I* **can** *buy anything I want.*

in the case of

A wordy construction, best avoided.

> X *In the* **case** *of your mother-in-law, she means well.*
> ✔ *Your mother-in-law means well.*

centre on/revolve around

Avoid "centre around," an illogical phrase.

comprises/comprised of

"Comprises" means "consists of." Do *not* use "is comprised of."

> X *Canada is comprised of ten provinces and two territories.*
> ✔ *Canada comprises ten provinces and two territories.*

conscious/conscience

"Conscious" is an adjective meaning "aware"; "conscience" is one's inner sense of morality.

The jury became increasingly **conscious** *of the criminal's lack of* **conscience**.

continual/continuous
"Continual" means "repeated"; "continuous" means "without ceasing."

Her homework was **continually** *interrupted by telephone calls from vacuum cleaner salesmen.*

The air conditioner was used **continuously** *throughout the long, hot day.*

could of/should of/would of
You mean "could have," "should have," "would have."

data/criteria/phenomena/media
All of these words are plural. Their singular forms are "datum," "criterion," "phenomenon," and "medium." Check the subject and verb agreement carefully with each.

Some people think the media **are** *responsible for all modern ills.*

disinterested/uninterested
"Disinterested" means "impartial"; "uninterested" means "bored" or "unconcerned."

The ideal referee is **disinterested** *in the outcome of the game, but shouldn't be* **uninterested** *in the actions of the players.*

due to
"Due to" is acceptable only after some form of the verb "to be." Use "because of" to imply a causal relationship.

The bus is **due to** *arrive in fifteen minutes.*

elicit/illicit
"To elicit" is a verb meaning to "evoke"; "illicit" is an adjective meaning "illegal."

The questions at the press conference should **elicit** *some response to the president's* **illicit** *behaviour.*

enthuse/enthused
Avoid these words. Use "enthusiastic" instead.

Bruce Springsteen's fans were **enthusiastic** *about his concert tour.*

equally as
Do not use "equally" and "as" together. Instead, use one or the other.

She and her brother are equally good at contact sports.

She is as good as her brother at contact sports.

etc.
Avoid this abbreviation, which usually means that the author does not know what else to say.

the fact that
Avoid this wordy expression.

factor
This word adds nothing; leave it out.

farther/further
"Farther" refers to actual distance; "further" is abstract.

> The **farther** he walked, the more his feet hurt.

> She would not stand for any **further** shenanigans.

fewer/less
"Fewer" is used with plural nouns; "less" is used with singular nouns.

> The **fewer** the guests, the **less** food we will need.

firstly/secondly,
"First" and "second" are all you really need.

hopefully
Replace this word with "It is hoped that."

> X **Hopefully**, the paper will be finished tomorrow.
> ✔ **It is hoped that** the paper will be finished tomorrow.

imply/infer
"To imply" means "to suggest"; "to infer" means "to conclude."

> She **implied** that he was cheap; he **inferred** that he should have offered to pay her bus fare.

into
Avoid using this preposition to mean "interested in."

> X He was **into** macrame.
> ✔ He was **interested in** macrame.

irregardless
This is wrong. The correct word is "regardless."

its/it's
"Its" is the possessive form, like "his" or "her." "It's" is a contraction for "it is" or "it has."

> That dog's bark is worse than **its** bite. **It's** certainly got big teeth, though.

-ize
Avoid verbs with this ending. There is usually a simpler form.

> X He **utilized** the facilities.
> ✔ He **used** the facilities.

lay/lie
"Lay" takes an object; "lie" does not.

*The farmer made the hen **lie** on the nest to **lay** an egg.*

like/as/as if

"Like" is a preposition and should not be used as a conjunction. Substitute "as" or "as if" if a clause follows.

> X *He looks **like** he's going to die.*
> ✔ *He looks **as if** he's going to die.*
> ✔ *He looks **like** death warmed over.*

myself

"Myself" is not a more polite form of "I" or "me." It should be reserved for use as an intensifier or reflexive.

> X *The hostess introduced my wife and myself to the guests.*
> ✔ *The hostess introduced my wife and me to the guests.*
> ✔ *I, myself, solved the problem.*
> ✔ *I drove myself to the airport.*

oriented/orientated

Avoid these words.

parameters/perimeters

Use "perimeters" to mean "boundaries." Avoid the use of "parameters" except in its specific application to geometry.

parent

Do not use this word as a verb; "parenting" is also suspect. "Parenthood" is a perfectly acceptable substitute.

practice/practise

"Practice" is the noun; "practise" is the verb.

> *I know **practice** makes perfect, but I hate to **practise**.*

presently

Substitute "currently" or "now."

principal/principle

The first means "chief" or "main" as an adjective, the head of a school as a noun; the second means "a basic truth."

> *His **principal** objection to her comments was that they were based on questionable **principles**.*

quote/quotation

"Quote" is a verb, *not* a noun—"quotation" is the noun.

> X *This **quote** from Richard Nixon makes the point clear.*
> ✔ *This **quotation** from Richard Nixon makes the point clear.*

relate to

Use this verb to indicate how one idea is related to another. Do not use it to mean "get along with."

> X *How do you relate to your new psychiatrist?*
> ✔ *This point relates directly to my argument.*

suppose to

Use "supposed to," or better, use "should" or "ought to."

that/which

Use "that" when what follows restricts the meaning. Use "which" in a non-restrictive case.

> *Here is the woman* **that** *I told you about.* (not just any woman, but a specific one)

> *His fortune,* **which** *included stock certificates, bonds, and the first penny he had ever earned, was kept in an old shoebox under his bed.* (the words surrounded by commas supply incidental, non-restrictive information)

their/there/they're

"Their" is possessive; "there" is an adverb or an expletive; "they're" is a contraction of "they are."

> **There** *ought to be a law against* **their** *foolishness.* **They're** *asking for trouble.*

try and

Replace this phrase with "try to."

> *We must* **try to** *stop meeting like this.*

unique

"Unique" means "one of a kind." It cannot be modified.

> X *Her sequined dress was* **very unique.**
> ✔ *Her sequined dress was* **unique**.

who's/whose

"Who's" is a contraction of "who is" or "who has"; "whose" is the possessive form.

> **Who's** *been sleeping in my bed?*

> **Whose** *bed is this, anyway?*

-wise

Avoid this suffix.

> X *Timewise, the project is on schedule.*
> ✔ *The project is on schedule.*

APPENDIX

The following is a list of sources of general information as well as sources pertaining to specific disciplines.

■ General Dictionaries

Gage Canadian Dictionary (1983)
The Oxford English Dictionary (1888–1928, Supplements)
Webster's Third New International Dictionary (1961)

■ Special Dictionaries

Dictionary of Modern English Usage (1965)
Roget's International Thesaurus (1977)

■ General Encyclopedias

The Canadian Encyclopedia (1985)
New Encyclopaedia Britannica (1985)

■ Special Encyclopedias and Reference Works

Biography
Canadian Who's Who (1910–)
Dictionary of American Biography (1927–80, Supplements)
Dictionary of Canadian Biography 1966–)
Dictionary of National Biography (1862–1958, Supplements)
International Who's Who (1935–)
Who's Who in America (1899–)

Fine arts
Encyclopedia of World Art (1959–1983)
Encyclopedia of World Architecture (1979)

History
Canadian Historical Review
An Encyclopedia of World History (1972)
Story, N. *The Oxford Companion to Canadian History and Literature* (1967, Supplement 1973)

Literature

Bartlett, John. *Familiar Quotations* (1980)
Cambridge History of American Literature (1960)
Cambridge History of English Literature (1907–33)
Contemporary Authors (1962–)
Essay and General Literature Index (1900–)
Granger's Index to Poetry (1982)
Hart, James D. *Oxford Companion to American Literature* (1983)
Harvey, Sir Paul. *Oxford Companion to Classical Literature* (1962)
———. *Oxford Companion to English Literature* (1967)
New Cambridge Bibliography of English Literature (1985)
Oxford Companion to Canadian Literature (1983)
Short Story Index (1974–)

Music

Encyclopedia of Music in Canada (1981)
The New Grove Dictionary of Music and Musicians (1980)
Thompson, Oscar. *International Cyclopedia of Music and Musicians* (1975)

Philosophy

Dictionary of the History of Ideas (1973–1974)
Encyclopedia of Philosophy (1967)

Social sciences

International Encyclopedia of the Social Sciences (1968–1979)
Handbook of Social Science Research (1979)
The Literature of Political Science (1969)
Sources of Information in the Social Sciences (1986)

Yearbooks (current information)

Britannica Book of the Year (1938–)
Canadian Almanac and Directory (1847–)
Canadian Annual Review (1960–)
Canadian News Facts (1967–)
Facts on File (1940–)
World Almanac and Book of Facts (1868–)

■ Periodical Indexes

Another excellent source of information is the periodical index. Often the periodical will give you more current material than is available in books. There are many indexes to supply you with the names of publications. The following list will help get you started. General indexes are indicated by a single asterisk (*). Indexes and abstracts available "on line" are indicated by double asterisks (**).

Abstracts of Popular Culture (1976–1982)
** *Art Index* (1929–)
American Humanities Index (1975–)
** *Biography Index (1949–)*
** *Book Review Digest* (1905–)
** *Business Periodicals Index* (1958–)
** *Canadian Business Index* (1975–)
** *Canadian Magazine Index* (1985–)
* ****** *Canadian Periodical Index* (1928–)
** *Humanities Index* (1974)
International Political Science Abstracts (1951–)
** *MLA International Bibliography of Books and Articles on the Modern Languages and Literatures* (1921–)
Music Index (1949–)
* ****** *New York Times Index* (1851–)
* *Poole's Index to Periodical Literature* (1802–1906) (subject guide only, but some libraries may have a separate author index)
Popular Periodical Index (1973–)
** *Psychological Abstracts (1927–)*
* ****** *Readers' Guide to Periodical Literature* (1900–)
* ****** *Social Sciences Index* (1974)
** *Sociological Abstracts* (1953–)

■ Guides to Documentation

American Psychological Association. *Publication Manual of the American Psychological Association*. 3rd ed. Washington: American Psychological Assn., 1983.

The Chicago Manual of Style. 13th ed. Chicago: U of Chicago P, 1982.

Gibaldi, Joseph, and Walter S. Achtert. *MLA Handbook for Writers of Research Papers*. 2nd ed. New York: Modern Language Association, 1984.

Hodges, John C., and Mary E. Whitten. *Harbrace College Handbook For Canadian Writers*. 2nd ed. Toronto: Harcourt Brace Jovanovich, Canada, 1986.

Turabian, Kate L. *A Manual for Writers of Term Papers, Theses, and Dissertations*. 4th ed. Chicago: U of Chicago P, 1973.

Wiles, Roy M. *Scholarly Reporting in the Humanities*. 4th ed. Toronto: U of Toronto P, 1979.

Index